FORMING A LITURGICAL CHOIR

A Practical Approach

Paolo Iotti

Translated by Patrick Lee

THE PASTORAL PRESS
Washington, DC

Translated by Patrick Lee from *Guidare un Coro Liturgico* Bologna: Edizioni Dehoniane Bologna, 1990.

Illustrations by Marco Deflorian.

Selections from the Constitution on the Sacred Liturgy, the General Instruction on the Roman Missal, and the General Instruction of the Liturgy of the Hours are reprinted from *Documents on the Liturgy 1963-1979: Conciliar, Papal, and Curial Texts*, Collegeville: The Liturgical Press, 1982.

ISBN: 1-56929-020-2

The Pastoral Press
225 Sheridan Street, N.W.
Washington, D.C. 20011
(202) 723-1254

The Pastoral Press is the publications division of the National Association of Pastoral Musicians, a membership organization of musicians and clergy dedicated to fostering the art of musical liturgy.

Printed in the United States of America

Contents

Foreword

This book began as a thesis submitted by Professor Paolo Iotti to the Istituto Superiore di Scienze Religiose Ss. Vitale e Agricola for the Degree of Master of Religious Sciences, Bologna, 1990. In its present form it has been translated, edited, and adapted for an English speaking readership by Patrick Lee in collaboration with Professor Iotti.

Although many parts of the book refer particularly to the place of the choir or other specialized groups of musicians and singers, it must be clearly understood that the primary musical role belongs to the assembly of the faithful. The first task for anyone engaged in making liturgical music is to enable the people to celebrate their true role in the liturgy with worthy music that is well performed. One of the major concerns of this book has been to encourage and to develop this vital aspect of our communal worship in a practical and prayerful way.

Musical terms familiar to readers in the United States have been used together with alternative terms more generally understood by English speaking musicians in other parts of the world. All musical examples have been especially chosen from sources readily available and familiar to the reader.

The Appendix has been redesigned to offer, in outline, a simple method of vocal training specifically related to the needs of English speaking singers.

Preface

The Role of the Liturgical Choir

"There are some who think that the liturgical revivial implies that choirs have had their day, that they have outlasted their usefulness and can quietly be scrapped . . . The principle upon which such action seeks to rest has no foundation in truth. If it is to be desired that the liturgical assembly be initiated, educated, and guided in its singing, a choir is indispensable. The choir, while adding dignity and solemnity by its own mastery of what it sings, must also undertake the moderating function of leading and sustaining the participation of the faithful in those parts which are proper to them."

The passage quoted above is taken from a letter of the Consilium ad Exequandam Constitutionem de Sacra Liturgia addressed to the Presidents of Conferences of Bishops in 1966.[1] It warns us against possibly misinterpreting the document of Vatican II about the role of the choir in the liturgy and the choir's relationship to the assembly. These documents do not propose abolishing the *schola cantorum* but give the choir a greater role, which must be one of service to the whole assembly.[2]

During the time of the Council, the anxieties of many priests and people led them to question the importance of the choir which was accused of appropriating, for its sole use, the singing within the liturgical celebration.

More recent thought on the role of music in liturgy underlines the immense richness of many of the 1966 intuitions. It is not a matter of "choir" or "no choir." What is important is to understand the true role of the choir, its choice of repertoire, and the way this repertoire is performed. The whole assembly, which includes the choir, must be able to celebrate God's glory together as one.

What is special to the choir is its task of adding to the celebration through effective performance. It must also guide and lead the assembly in an adequate fashion. It must support the singing but not dominate; it must work with and assist the whole praying community in its worship.

In order to achieve all aims, a choir must be musically competent and know how to sing. Liturgically, it must be aware of it's role and the nature of the assembly it serves. For itself, the choir must appreciate that it is more than merely a group of musicians performing a work; it must realize that it is an integral part of a group of Christians united in praising God.

The Liturgical Choir: A Definition

A certain ambiguity exists; what does the term "liturgical choir" mean? The word "choir," in the old ecclesiastical sense, usually meant a group of singers who performed polyphonic music, usually with mixed voices. Obviously such choirs sang liturgical music, but were they really liturgical choirs?

To define what a liturgical choir is we will not take as the main criterion the repertoire that is performed; rather, we will ask what kind of function the vocal group serves during the liturgical celebration. By "liturgical choir" we mean any group of singers which has the task of initiating, educating, and leading the assembly in singing and which helps to achieve a degree of solemnity and beauty in the worship, thereby helping the faithful to pray in an atmosphere of joy. By this definition even a small group of people technically incapable of performing polyphonic music can be considered a true liturgical choir when they honestly serve the community of which they are part.

According to this perspective, we have to understand that the training of the choir director needs to go beyond musical skills. Musical competence is, of course, important, but we know from experience that the possession of only musical skills can be an obstacle to the liturgical development of the community. Anyone interested in liturgical music must be capable of choosing and performing music and songs appropriate to the rites and to the needs of the people celebrating these rites. Briefly, as the Council stressed, a firm foundation in faith, theoretical knowledge, and genuine liturgical training are essential for singers and composers.[3] But this is not enough. The choir director, a crucial figure with a special task to perform, needs those psychological and pedagogical skills which will ensure that the liturgical music is truly fruitful and goes beyond just the music itself.

Competence of the Choir Director

Let us analyze more fully the various skills a choir director requires. They are musical, liturgical, psychological, and pedagogical skills. It may seem easier to treat these individually. Actually the choir director needs to combine, in a unique manner, considerable training in a variety of closely related disciplines. If we discuss these skills separately, it is because of the necessity for education, at a profound level, in a number of differing fields. Although the liturgical choir is basically a group formed to make music, an understanding of liturgy by the choir director is equally as important as any musical expertise. In addition, the director's education is incomplete without some knowledge of the basic psychological principles of group dynamics.

Notes

1. Translation from *Documents on the Liturgy 1963-1979: Conciliar, Papal, and Curial Texts* (Collegeville: The Liturgical Press, 1982) 124.
2. See Constitution on the Sacred Liturgy, articles 112-118, 121.
3. See ibid., articles 115-121.

1

Musical Competence

"Competence" is here understood as the possession of a number of gifts, skills, qualities, knowledge, and experiences required to achieve a goal. It is clear that a natural disposition and a special ability to "feel" the music are necessary. Study and experience can help to develop many of these attributes and may also reveal hitherto hidden talents and unexpected enthusiasms. We will now analyze these specifically musical skills.

The Vocal Instrument

In any discussion about competence, the first consideration must be how to make the best use of the voice. Where the singers cannot read music (a situation all too common), it falls to the leader or director to teach, by example, not only the melody but also tonal color and interpretation.

Singing well is possible only if we constantly strive to improve. The voice does not exist in the abstract; we have to accept the voice we have, excellent, good or mediocre, for what it is and work to improve it. Here it may help to refer to the notes about vocalization contained in the Appendix where some insights into the anatomy of the voice, breath control, and the positioning of vowels and consonants are offered. There are also exercises to discover and improve the placing of the voice as well as suggestions about the classification of voices.

Other General Competencies

The ability to read music accurately and quickly, at least in the treble (G) and bass (F) clefs in which most choral music is written, is a basic requirement. Developing this skill might well be linked to learning to play a particular musical instrument. More about this will be considered in a later chapter.

It is also very useful, if not absolutely vital, to know something of the rules of classical harmony so that various passages may be suitably adapted to the choir's ability. When we make such adaptations, faithfulness to the composer's intentions is important, and for this reason a good general, historical, musical background is required. In addition, some knowledge of genre, form, and style in a wider context than what is known as "sacred music" is needed.

Is There a Christian Music as Such?

We need to be precise about the term "sacred music." Like any widely used expression, this expression, in turn, has become too general in its meaning. The term "sacred music" is used to identify any music having links with Christianity. Even more, we tend to assume that such music is Christian music. To avoid any misunderstanding, we would define the term, for our purposes, as "ritual music of the Christian people" through which believers celebrate the liturgy.

If we admit that such Christian music exists, then it will be the kind of music that has a primary and unique place in the liturgical celebration, regardless of other cultural concerns springing from the environment in which the celebration is embedded. It would be dangerous to assume, for instance, that a mass sung by a four-part choir was the more sacred because it created a harmony that raised the soul to God. Any idea that the function of the music was to heighten the emotional aspects of the celebration risks creating a false notion that true prayer is dependent upon emotion.

Actually, an historical analysis of the inter-relationship of music, liturgy, and culture reveals that a music that is holy, liturgical, Christian, or profane of itself, does not exist. The Christian people do not possess a particular "sacred" music, but they have used—and still use—many various kinds of music, according to their individual tastes. There is always a close link between music used in liturgy and the music of the surrounding culture. The musical language of the Christian worship has come out of— and still derives from—the different cultures where the message has been announced. A consequence of poor historical, liturgical, and musical education can be to assume that music, originating in very different times and very dissimilar social circumstances, is suitable for today. This is not to say that we must not use music from the past . . . on the contrary. However, we must realize that if we want to use such time-honored music like a Latin motet, we must prepare the conditions carefully so that the piece is understood and so that it meets the needs of the rite in which it is used.

Features of Christian Ritual Music

Here we face a major problem. What type of training is required to ensure that the music chosen can adequately meet the needs of our choir and our assembly? What are the main criteria to be considered? Over and above the choir director's musical and liturgical education, we must note that Christian, ritual music has two particular features: it belongs to the whole community, as does the liturgy itself; and in it the words play a specific part.

In making any choice the choir leader must bear in mind these two general ideas. If we should wish to use music from the ancient traditions but music that cannot be readily understood in the modern context, we should do so only after an adequate introduction, explanation, and justification have been offered. Too often there are choirs, for instance, that sing during the communion without involving the assembly. When this happens, the people celebrating are not helped to become fully involved in the event which should integrate music, liturgy, and prayer. Frequently the choice is made on the basis of some individual taste or because the piece is used in another church or community.

To verify the competence of the choir director in liturgical music, G.M. Rossi, in an article in *Musica e Assemblea* proposes an interesting "examination of conscience":

- Am I aware of my task?
- Do I believe that I am a good director of liturgical music only because I am a good musician?
- Do I understand the demands of the liturgy, and have I ever read those texts concerning my work which are contained in the various documents of the church?
- If I have felt unprepared, have I ever thought that someone might be able to give me a hand in either the liturgical or musical aspects of my work?
- Am I concerned to prepare for celebrations in a rational manner and in accordance with the norms expressed in the General Instruction on the Roman Missal? No. 73 says: "The ceremonies, as also the musical and pastoral arrangements, for every liturgical celebration, should be prepared with care and the co-operation of those concerned. They should work together under the leadership of the rector of the church and should take into account the wishes of the people concerning the parts which pertain to the congregation."
- Do I search for an adequate repertoire for both the choir and the assembly, and do I love the dialogue between choir and congregation? Do I understand the importance of this dialogue or do I refuse or, even worse, avoid it?
- Do I first consider the aesthetic point of view and prefer those festivals at which the choir has a paramount role and the assembly does nothing?[1]

This last point is important and must be examined more closely.

Aesthetic Criteria for a Liturgical Musical Language

In the formation of choir directors, the conservatories consider aesthetic perfection, through correct interpretation, as the principle merit even though the aesthetic concepts vary from age to age. In church we should not look for musical perfection for its own sake, but through the music we should strive to support and to reinforce the gospel message in all its forms. We should give to the profession of faith and the prayer of the church a deeper meaning which reinforces the solemnity of the liturgy in all its actions and words. Liturgical music is capable of functioning in a way that achieves these aims without reaching those high levels of performance traditionally understood as "art."

Liturgy demands that we replace an aesthetic of beauty for its own sake with an aesthetic that looks first toward the function and purpose of music in worship. "A mere artistic realization which implies strict observance of signs and expression marks of an earlier age is insufficient."[2]

Going beyond an aesthetic of "beauty for its own sake" does not mean accepting carelessness or lack of precision in performance. Neither should participation by the assembly be used to excuse poor musical execution; the involvement of the people should not mean we are to accept the banal.

If we are to serve the community at prayer, the principle aesthetic problem is different. In which way can the style of the music enhance the assembly's union with God and its imitation of Christ in everyday life? We do not wish to be overly ambitious, but it must be accepted that singing is prayer.

To be more concrete, music is an element within the pattern of celebration; what is being celebrated and what aspects need to be stressed must be considered. As well as the music, other elements are involved; words, gestures, silences, light, the congregation, etc. The "right" music is that which is best suited to convey the desired message. The "right" music is that which responds to the needs of the community and underlines and deepens certain aspects of its members' relationship with the Almighty and with each other.

"The reference model for a music in tune with the liturgy is not the Gregorian chant but one which is fully symbolic of the mystery as it is celebrated in our time, and which is music meant to offer a model of clarity (as, in its own time and place, Gregorian monody certainly was)."[3]

The future of any active involvement of the assembly in the music of the liturgy is dependent upon these general concepts and operational guidelines being taken to heart by all who work in the field of liturgical music (composers, choir directors, singers, animators, and instrumentalists).

"If one of the main causes of the gap waiting to be filled is the lack of understanding of the reforms, identified by the Episcopal Commission for the Liturgy in 1983, then now is the time to put things right by the proper liturgical formation of those who are responsible for the music in the liturgy."[4]

Notes

1. G.M. Rossi, "Coro e assemblea I," *Musica e Assemblea* 1 (1984) 50, 18-19.

2. J.-Y. Hameline, "L'arte del coro liturgico," in *L'arte del popolo celebrante, atti della settimana internazionale organizzata da Universa Laus "Psalitte Sapienter" Pamplona, 28.8-2.9 1967* (Torino-Leumann: LDC, 1968) 91.

3. F. Rainolda, "Il Documento UL '80 nello sviluppo storico da Pio X ad oggi," *Rivista Liturgica* (1981) 1, 28-56.

4. G. Agamennone, "Se cè solo il coro addio," in *La musica sacra e il nostro tempo* (Torino-Leumann: LDC, 1986) 114.

2

Liturgical Competence

We must distinguish between two levels of liturgical competence: the first, necessary but insufficient of itself, concerns the technical knowledge of the rites and ceremonies of the church. This knowledge must also include an awareness of the rubrics— a technical-liturgical competence. The second level, which implies a deeper liturgical understanding, is achieved only when the technical knowledge is informed by a truly Christian awareness that the liturgy is the *culmen et fons*, the "starting point" and the "point of arrival" from which we always receive fresh energy and renewed motivation.[1]

Liturgical Ministry and Personal Committment

As the pastoral message from the Italian bishops stated in 1983, a genuine competence in liturgy must be characterized by a real faith which is expressed in commitment to a ministry of service to the liturgical assembly:

> For an awareness of what is a true liturgical ministry it is necessary to understand that with competence must go an interior involvement in what is done . . . because liturgy and the Christian life are intimately connected and a ministry in the liturgy must demonstrate an adequate commitment to the life of the church and the faithful.[2]

Helping the Assembly Celebrate: A Service

Helping others celebrate their faith in music calls for an interior, spiritual growth on the part of the musician: without it we run the risk of considering the musical aspects of the celebration more important than the celebration itself. The choir director who presents or sings a "sung Mass" as a concert puts the celebration of the risen Lord into second place.

Rather, as was stressed at the beginning of this work, the task of both the choir director and the choir is to lead the assembly in the singing and to involve it in active participation. To achieve this aim, a repertoire, suited to the needs of the assembly, must be chosen; it must also be within their technical capacity. At the same time we must not deceive ourselves that an appropriate choice will bring about real participation: only a process of continual education can help to bring about the desired personal involvement. However, the choir and its director cannot achieve these objectives on their own: the practical preparation of every liturgy should involve priests, readers, and servers as well as the choir and its director. "The liturgical music which is taught to the choir and to the congregation should have been chosen to fit the framework of a clearly defined pastoral plan of action." In this way the celebrant will be in a position where he is able, for example in the homily, to refer to, even to study in depth or to examine in a general way, the content of the music because the assembly will have been asked to sing music that fits the context of the celebration.

In 1988 the Piedmont Conference of Bishops, writing about the role of the choir in the liturgy, said:

> The chants and the music are a part of the whole and therefore it would be a mistake to limit them to the choir alone as if the choir's task was merely concerned with technical or ornamental aspects of the celebration. It is a serious error to see the rite

and the music as two parallel roads. In fact the chants and other music form an integral part of the liturgy and must be seen as such.[3]

The choir director who is called to share with others the selection of liturgical music should not feel in any way inferior. On the contrary, it should be realized that working with a team calls for the exercise of those special gifts which have been placed at the service of the community.

Attitudes toward Service and Competence.

Choir directors are required to have not only the necessary musical techniques but also knowledge and understanding of the rites and rubrics. These may seem to be obvious qualifications, but such skills do not always appear to be as highly regarded as one would wish; perhaps because people do not wish to be too critical of others. But here lies a danger: simple willingness and an ability to improvise are not always virtues, especially in the field of liturgical music. The Constitution on the Sacred Liturgy (art. 115) recognized this and insisted upon proper musical instruction in all places of learning such as seminaries, novitiates, church schools etc.

Although it would require several years of study to examine fully the complexities of either the musical or the liturgical demands, we want to look at certain fundamentals of music and liturgy without which it is impossible to offer an adequate service to the community.

Technical Liturgical Competence

If we are to understand the various meanings of the word "rite," we need to know how the music is enshrined within a rite, how it becomes a rite in itself; we also need to examine the relationship between rite, music, and the assembly.

Rite: A General Definition and Special Features

In general, we understand "rite" as a gesture or series of gestures that possess a religious or sacred significance. For instance, we have the "rite of Mass" which, in turn, is made up of a number of distinct "rites"—the introductory rites, the rite of peace, the concluding rites.

In the General Instruction on the Roman Missal (no. 7) we read:

> In Mass or the Lord's Supper, the people of God are called together, with a priest presiding and acting in the person of Christ, to celebrate the memorial of the Lord or eucharistic sacrifice." Here the word "memorial" does not point to a mere commemoration but to the authentic presence of Jesus, in the celebration today, at his Last Supper, Passion, Death and Resurrection. In celebrating this "memorial" the people of God use gestures and signs; together these gestures and signs constitute the Rite of the Mass.

This same section also maintains that in the post-conciliar liturgy the celebrant is not solely the priest: it is the whole people of God, the people who, presided over by the priest, accomplish the act of celebration. This is why God's people must "sing the Mass" and not sing "during the Mass"; the assembly's act of singing is not something added to or omitted from the celebration at will.

At this point it would be well to remember that not only the eucharistic sacrifice but every liturgy is made up of actions and signs, and through them the assembly celebrates Christ's presence: "Wherever two or three are gathered together in my name there am I in the midst of them" (Mt 18:20).

Let us now examine the common elements making up a rite. The celebrating community seeks to express that union with God and that following of Christ which give value and depth of meaning to life. The community does this through familiar gestures and signs which are part of its everyday experience. In use, these very ordinary signs and symbols assume a deeper significance and transcend a simply prosaic understanding.

Rite, Music, and Singing

Among the actions, pride of place is given to the music and especially to those parts of the Mass which should, properly, be sung, i.e., the chants. When the people of God are celebrating together, they do so as a joyful community and this joy expresses itself not though the simple word alone but through the word that was sung.

The community, the celebration, and the music are interwoven realities: the community gives life to the celebration whereas the celebration draws the community together. A joyful community sings and in singing expresses its joy. But the focalized actions and signs must be brought alive each time if they are to link the rite with people's lives

The ritual celebration demands faithfulness to the tradition from which the actions and symbols have been derived. It also requires creative ability to give life to each and every celebration. This is why when we prepare liturgical music we must abide by the rubrics and yet possess an essential, operational creativity that is aware of the special needs of the particular assembly. As Cardinal Martini maintains:

> The rubrics must envisage a constant and demanding creativity. In fact, there are texts that require making choices and, as a consequence, must be approached with a degree of creativity. Such creativity does not mean pure invention but calls for sensitive interpretation. This creativity must bring to life the prescribed texts.[4]

It is not necessary for us, as choir directors, to be always introducing new music. We should be ready to use old, traditional settings and music when appropriate, but we must sing them with a new heart and with the enthusiasm of one who sings a joyful song.

The relationship between faithfulness to tradition and creativity in the context of liturgy is a profound one. However let us examine three ritual schemes as they operate within our communities: at Mass, and at morning prayer and evening prayer where there are similarities. Briefly, we need to understand the part music plays in our celebrations.

Let us look at the ritual pattern of the Mass with close reference to the General Instruction on the Roman Missal (GIRM).

Introductory Rites

These comprise the entrance antiphon (Introit), a greeting, the penitential rite, the appeal for mercy (*Kyrie*), the Glory to God (*Gloria*) when the season allows, and the opening prayer (Collect). The purpose of these rites is to prepare the assembly to hear and to attend to the readings, namely, the liturgy of the word and to celebrate, in a dignified manner, the sacrifice of the Body and Blood of Christ, that is, the liturgy of the eucharist (GIRM 24).

LITURGY OF EUCHARIST

INTRODUCTORY RITES	LITURGY OF WORD	PREPARATION RITE	EUCHARISTIC PRAYER	COMMUNION RITE	CONCLUDING RITE
Entrance Procession and Song	*1st Reading*	Preparation of Altar	Preface	*Lord's Prayer*	Announcements
Veneration of Altar	*Psalm Response*	Procession-Presentation of Gifts, and Song	Holy, Holy	Rite of Peace	Greeting
Sign of Cross	*2nd Reading*	Placing Gifts on Altar with Accompanying Prayers	Epiclesis	*Breaking of Bread and Lamb of God*	*Blessing*
Greeting	Gospel Acclamation and Procession	Mixing of water and wine "Lord God, we . . ."	Institution Narrative	Commingling	*Dismissal*
Introduction	*Gospel*	Incensation	Memorial Acclamation	Private Preparation	Veneration of Altar
Penitential Rite or Sunday Renewal of Baptism	*Homily*	Washing of hands	Anamnesis	Invitation	
(Lord Have Mercy)	Creed		Offering	*Communion Procession and Song*	
Glory to God	*General Intercessions*	*Prayer over Gifts*	Intercessions	Silent Prayer/ Song of Praise	
Opening Prayer			Doxology	*Prayer after Communion*	
Helping people become a celebrating community	Listening-responding to God's word in song, speech, and silence	A simple preparation of table, gifts, and community	Praise-thanksgiving for gifts of creation and salvation	Participation in Heavenly Banquet	Conclusion-Beginning Mission
Gathering				Sharing	
Mood-setting				Unity	

Major elements within rites are italicized.

Although the eucharistic prayer is essentially one, its sections are listed individually.

The **entrance antiphon** is sung while the ministers make their way to the sanctuary. It may be performed by the choir and people in alternation, or by a cantor and people in like manner, or even by the people alone. The Instruction, as a final solution, allows the antiphon to be sung by the choir alone. The aim of this chant, which with the offertory and the communion pieces may be called "processionals," is to unite the assembly in a spirit of celebration. The singing should accompany the rite—the procession of the priests and ministers to the altar. It should not continue beyond the action; otherwise, there is danger of it becoming singing for the sake of singing and failing in its true purpose.

Chants that can, if necessary, be curtailed should be chosen, but the value of this entrance antiphon in drawing the people together must be stressed. The procession of the priest toward the sanctuary is more than just a simple movement from the sacristy to the altar; it is a symbol of another movement, that of the People of God, represented by their presider, the priest, toward the two tables of the Lord, that of the word and that of the eucharist (GIRM 25, 26).

The **greeting** consists of a welcome and an introduction to the theme of the celebration. The **penitential rite** is an invitation to repent. This is followed, if it has not been included in the rite, by the Lord have mercy.

The **Kyrie** is an acclamation by which we ask for forgiveness, and its singing must not be left to the choir. It is an appeal that must be made by everybody, the people, choir, and cantor all taking part in it (GIRM 30).

The **Glory to God**, the *Gloria*, is a song of acclamation and invocation. The General Instruction describes it as a hymn that should be performed by the whole congregation, or else by the congregation alternating with the choir. In the last resort it may be sung by the choir alone but obviously, when this is done, the assembly is denied a powerful means of their rightful expression (GIRM 31). In the pre-conciliar Mass (the Missal of Pius V) the singing of the *Gloria* could continue till the *Credo!* Validity resided in the priest reciting it to himself. It is impossible to reconcile this view with that of the missal approved by Pope Paul VI, where it says: "it is God's people who celebrate the rite and as a result they must be able to express themselves using their particular talents and skills."

The Glory to God is to be sung or said on the Sundays outside Advent and Lent, on Solemnities and Feast Days, and at solemn celebrations.

The **collect** is a unique prayer which comes after the people, at the invitation of the priest, have observed a short silence; the prayer of everyone is "collected" in this public utterance (GIRM 32).

Liturgy of the Word

The liturgy of the word is divided into three readings: normally the first is from the **Old Testament,** the second from the **New Testament,** and the final one from the **Gospel.** During the Easter Season the Old Testament readings are replaced by readings from the Acts of the Apostles.

After the first reading the assembly is invited to respond in the **responsorial psalm,** which is so called because it contains a response repeated by the people as a refrain. The psalm has a poetic structure and should be sung by everyone except when it is sung "directly" without a refrain (GIRM 36).

In the light of this last exception, there are two ways in which the psalm can be sung; it can be sung by a soloist against a musical accompaniment or the whole assembly can sing a song that substitutes for the psalm itself. These two choices must be used sparingly; first, because the symbolism of the dialogue would be lost and second, because to replace the responsorial psalm regularly would suggest that it is not as important a part of the liturgy of the word as the General Instruction very clearly says it is (GIRM 36).

In order to involve the people more fully, certain psalms and responses have been chosen to be used at various times and seasons instead of those given in the lectionary, provided that the psalm is in fact sung. For the same reason we may also sing the dialogue at the end of each reading.

The **gospel acclamation** Alleluia, except during Lent when alternative acclamation are used, comes from the Hebrew and means "Praise the Lord." It is a joyful cry, an outburst of happiness and gratitude that the word of the Lord is present in the life of the community. It is a chant, full of hope and trust in the Good News at every difficult time. Alleluia is an acclamation which conveys far more than the literal translation of the word;

for this reason it cannot be simply recited. The General Instruction states that "if the psalm after the reading is not sung, it is to be recited. If not sung, the *Alleluia* or the verse before the gospel may be omitted" (GIRM 39).

The choir director must ensure that not only the choir sings this chant. The Alleluia is part of the rite and should not be regarded as something to be listened to. It may, however, be elaborated: at Christmas or Easter, for example, at first it may be sung reponsorially with the choir, and then the choir may add harmonies under the people's part.

The liturgy of the word is completed by the **homily** and, on Sundays and at solemn celebrations, affirmed by the **profession of faith** (or creed) which is the people's assent and response to the scripture readings. Twice the General Instruction refers to the creed being "said," but it may be sung either by all, together or in alternation. Arising from their faith, the people exercise their priestly function in the **prayer of the faithful** or the **general intercessions**. These are not the prayers of the priest or of any "guide-book," but of the people.

Liturgy of the Eucharist

The liturgy of the eucharist begins with the **presentation of the gifts** in which the assembly brings the bread and wine to the altar and the priest prepares them for their offering to God in the eucharistic prayer. "The procession bringing the gifts is accompanied by the presentation song, which continues at least until the gifts have been placed on the altar" (GIRM 50). This part of the rite must be shared by all because the offering is identified with the giving of ourselves to the Lord. "In the eucharistic prayer thanks is given to God for the whole work of salvation and the gifts of bread and wine become the body and blood of Christ" (GIRM 48).

It is fitting that these processional songs or chants should be inspired by the liturgy of the day or the central themes of the readings. Hymns that express and reflect the spiritual idea of "offering" are also appropriate. It may be possible to sing the response, "Blessed be God forever." Always the participation of the assembly must be kept to the fore.

The *eucharistic prayer*, which begins with the preface in which we give thanks to God, includes general and specific expressions of thanksgiving, an acclamation, a first invocation of the power of God (epiclesis), the institution narrative, and the prayer of remembrance of the passion, death and resurrection of Christ (anamnesis). It continues with a further invocation of the Holy Spirit and with intercessions that express the union of the whole church, in heaven and on earth, in prayers for the living and dead. It concludes with the doxology which glorifies and praises God through, with and in Christ in the unity of the Holy Spirit.

It is of primary importance that the parts of this great prayer specifically belonging to the assembly should not be taken from them. These elements are the "Holy, holy" (*Sanctus*), the acclamation after the words of institution and the Great Amen. Ideally all three should be sung; the words preceding the "Holy, holy" explicitly require that the *Sanctus* be sung.

The **communion rite** consists of the **Lord's Prayer**, which may be sung by all; a development of the prayer (the embolism); another doxology spoken or sung by the people; the prayer for and the sign of peace; the hymn for the breaking of bread (*Agnus Dei*) and the distribution of holy communion.

There is no general directive as to how the **rite of peace** should be conducted; but such a directive exists for the "Lamb of God" which "is as a rule sung by the choir or cantor with the congregation responding" (GIRM 56e).

There is a question that needs consideration in regard to the **"breaking of bread."** In our normal Sunday celebration the breaking of the bread is reduced to the division of a single host; the symbolism of this fraction is, at best, diminished; although the General Instruction, by implication, expects it to take some time: "This invocation may be repeated as often as necessary to accompany the breaking of the bread. The final reprise concludes with the words, *grant us peace*" (GIRM 56e). The "action" or "gesture" is clearly associated with the singing.

After the people have been reconciled to God and to their brothers and sisters, they approach the altar to receive holy communion. During the reception of the sacrament the **communion antiphon or song** is sung; its purpose is "to express outwardly the communicants' union in spirit by means of the unity of their voices, to give evidence of joy of heart, and to make the procession to receive Christ's body more fully an act of community" (GIRM 56i). For this reason the song should, as far as possible, be linked to the themes of the liturgy of the word, to the homily, and to the other pirces sung. Although this song may be sung by the choir, the strong symbolism of us singing together as we go forward to meet Christ cannot be too strongly urged. As the procession ends, the singing should give way to prayerful silence (GIRM 56i). During the pause and as an alternative to silence "a hymn, psalm, or other song of praise may be sung by the entire congregation" (GIRM 56j).

Sometimes this hymn or psalm is understood as a thanksgiving after communion. In fact, the postcommunion prayers emphasize not thanksgiving, but zeal and determination to live according to God's will as expressed in the mysteries just celebrated. In Christ we have seen the inseparable link between the Last Supper and his readiness to follow the will of the Father. In any singing at this point we should be looking to unite ourselves with the life of Christ and acceptance of God's will for us. We should strive to link the liturgy we celebrate with the realities of daily life, and our song should reflect this in an appropriate manner.

Concluding Rite

The **blessing** and the final injunction to serve Christ in the world conclude the Mass. But what of a final song or recessional hymn? Neither the Order of Mass nor the General Instruction anticipate singing, and it seems illogical to do so after being dismissed. Nevertheless, there are some especially solemn times when some further, symbolic statement may be required. Whatever is chosen must be suited to the occasion and should contribute to the particular atmosphere. It may be to help the dispersal of the people, and choral or instrumental music could be used. In all events, it should take into account that some people may well be continuing their prayers.

Not Only the Mass

Any activity in which the whole body of the church takes part together is an occasion to meet Christ and to grow in faith. In reality "liturgical activity" is often understood as "celebrating Mass," and although the Mass is the highest expression of Christian celebration it is not the only form. All who are concerned with pastoral, liturgical, and catechetical work, might strive to make the occasions of their meeting together moments for communal prayer, alternatives to the Mass. Opportunities exist, and it is also possible to create new patterns of celebration.

If such gatherings wish to use alternative forms of prayer but feel a desire to join in the prayer of the universal church, they could use the divine office. The General Instruction on the Liturgy of the Hours (GILH), after saying that "sacred ministers have the liturgy of the hours entrusted to them in . . . a particular way" (GILH 28) goes on to say that "other religious communities and their individual members are advised to celebrate some parts of the liturgy of the hours . . . for it is the prayer of the Church and makes the whole Church, scattered throughout the world, one in heart and mind. This recommendation applies also to laypersons" (GILH 32).

Hopefully, choir directors will experience this need to pray the prayer of the church. At the least they should be technically prepared to direct the music of the office. It is also right to recall that this technical knowledge of rites and instructions does not constitute necessary liturgical competence.

The two most important elements of the liturgy of the hours are lauds and vespers, more commonly known today as morning prayer and evening prayer. In the following paragraphs we shall examine them first in a general way, and then with reference to the place and function of music in the celebration.

The Ritual Pattern of Morning Prayer and Evening Prayer

MORNING PRAYER	EVENING PRAYER
Opening Acclamation	Opening Acclamation
Hymn	Hymn
Psalm	Psalm
Psalm-prayer	Psalm-prayer
Old Testament Canticle	Psalm
Psalm	Psalm-prayer
Psalm-prayer	New Testament Canticle
Reading	Reading
Responsory	Responsory
Canticle of Zechariah	Canticle of Mary
Intercessions	Intercessions
Our Father	Our Father
Prayer	Prayer

"They [the sacred ministers] should, first and foremost, attach due importance to those hours that are, so to speak, the two hinges of the liturgy of the hours, that is, morning prayer and evening prayer, which should not be omitted except for a serious reason" (GILH 29).

Lauds "celebrated as it is as the light of a new day dawning . . . recalls the resurrection of the Lord Jesus, the true light . . ." (GILH 38). At vespers we give thanks for the day and call to mind our redemption as we remember the Last Supper and Our Lord's sacrifice. The structure of both prayers is similar; the *Benedictus* is characteristic of lauds and the *Magnificat* of vespers.

The person who presides at the celebration, and who need not be in Holy Orders, begins with an acclamation: "Lord, open our lips" or "O God, come to our aid." These together with their responses may be sung. Then a hymn, an important musical feature, is sung. Its purpose is to express, in an easy and joyful manner, the particular feature of the hour, the day, the season, or the feast (GILH 41). A hymn in the breviary may be used or any other chant or poem, perhaps declaimed, that helps create a prayerful atmosphere. The hymn should not be sung antiphonally.

After the hymn comes the psalmody, made up of two psalms and a canticle. Lauds begins with a morning psalm followed by an Old Testament Canticle and then the third psalm, traditionally one of praise. At vespers the sequence is different; the two psalms or two sections of a longer psalm are followed by a New Testament Canticle.

The psalms are ancient Jewish religious poetry. Although not always directly addressed to God, they include hymns of praise, supplication, and thanksgiving. They are the work of many different authors, but tradition attributes some of the earliest psalms to the great King David.

In content the psalms express the mystery of salvation achieved by the God of the Exodus who constantly appears to people, speaks to them, and gives a transcendental significance to all their individual and social experiences. If we view the psalms from a New Testament perspective, we realize that they concern God's complete revelation to humankind in Christ.

The psalms are not readings nor were they specifically composed as prayers, but as poems of praise. Though sometimes they may be proclaimed like a reading, nevertheless, because of their literary character, they are rightly called in the Hebrew "Tehillim," that is, "songs of praise," and in the Greek "Psalmoi," "songs to be sung to the sound of the harp." In all the psalms there is a certain musical quality which determines the correct way of praying them. Therefore, though a psalm may be recited without being sung even by an individual in silence, its musical character should not be overlooked. While certainly offering a text to our mind, the psalm is more concerned with moving the spirits of those singing and listening, and indeed of those accompanying it with music. (GILH 103)

Clearly, the link between music and psalm cannot be broken; yet the particular ways in which the music of the psalms may be performed are many, and not all of them can be defined as "psalmody." Technically, psalmody is a special genre which is not a simple way "to make music with the voice" nor to exploit a musical resource to give value to the word. The specific technique of psalmody is what is known as "cantillation"; this method of vocalizing lies between ordinary speech and real song.

When we come to study, with our choir, ways of singing the psalms in the divine office, we must pay particular attention to this unique combination of music and word; we must remember that the first must always be interpreted with regard to the second. Singing the psalms may not always be aesthetically satisfying in terms of "beautiful music," but it can be more fully appreciated when we realize that, through music, we are contributing to a clearer understanding of the word of the Lord by those who are celebrating together.

We are now ready to consider some of the different ways, not all them technically psalmody, in which the psalms may be sung:

Free melodies such as we hear in the Gregorian chant introits, in the Renaissance polyphonic compositions, in the choruses and arias by Monteverdi, Vivaldi, and Marcello among others from the Baroque period (roughly 1580 to 1760) through to the present day in the works of composers like Perosi.

The **strophic hymn** in which the psalm is arranged in strictly metrical form, allowing it to be sung to any matching metrical hymn tune.

The **melodic recitative** which may be similar to psalmody but is too close to a musical art form.

Genuine psalmody is, as has already been stressed, cantillation and not mere chant. Psalmody is more an oral expression than a musical one; it is an enunciation that should allow the word to "grasp" or enfold the people who are praying. It has a particular verbal and temporal structure which is, at once, immersion and emission—a "baptism in the word." The differing forms of psalmody each have individual features; the most common of these may be categorized as follows:

• **Direct form** where the psalm is proclaimed by a soloist. Here, when the psalmist has become fully aware of the "message," the effect can lead to contemplation of certain aspects of the psalm or special reference to its content. The simplest of psalm tones, which allow for an expressive declamation similar to the poetic recitation of a literary passage, seems most suitable for this form.

• **The refrain form** in which the psalmist sings phrases or short verses of the psalm, and the assembly responds with a refrain (e.g., Psalm 135, "O give thanks to the Lord for he is good," with the refrain "Great is his love, love without end" [Joseph Gelineau]).

• **The responsorial form** which is familiar to us from its use in the liturgy of the word. Here an antiphon that sums up the message of the psalm text is inserted between the verses.

• **Alternation** is the most traditional method of psalmody. Performed by two groups, soloist/assembly, choir/assembly, or either side of the church, each group takes its turn in singing alternate sections or verses of the psalm. For this type of psalmody the appropriate models of cantillation are the classical Gregorian or other psalm tones.

• **Mixed Forms** offer yet further opportunities for variation. A judicious mingling of any of the previous forms may be used. It may also be useful to alternate between singing and speaking.

Among all these forms of chant or psalmody, what do we choose? Whatever our choice, due account must be taken of the literary genre of the psalm, its length, its language, and its style. It is important to include opportunities for silent meditation, and a way should be found to enable those who pray the psalms to appreciate more easily their spiritual and literary flavor (GILH 121). Where there is difficulty deciding which of the various formats might be used, the first consideration should be given to the literary genre of the psalm. It may happen that a musical setting is not the most appropriate. "Thus the wisdom psalms and the narrative psalms are perhaps better listened to, whereas psalms of praise and thanksgiving are of their nature designed for singing in common" (GILH 279).

From what has been said about psalmody in the liturgy of the hours, it is clear that the choir director cannot present the psalms in a merely mechanical or repetitive fashion. Nor should they be regarded as easy or less demanding musically. On the contrary, with close study and constant reappraisal, singing or saying the psalms can offer moments of genuine creativity.

After the psalmody there is the short reading which varies according to the liturgical day, season, or feast. A longer reading may be used especially for celebration with the people (see GILH 45-46). However, short or long, these "readings are not of themselves designed for singing" (GILH 283). On the other hand, music could be used during the silence for meditation after either the reading or the homily.

The rite envisages a short responsory as an answer to the reading. This responsory, if it is not sung, may be omitted. There is freedom here for the choir director to use alternative music provided that it is of a similar type and purpose and allows the people to respond to the word (see GILH 49).

The Gospel canticle is now solemnly recited. The Canticle of Zechariah (the *Benedictus*) is by ancient tradition used at morning prayer; in this canticle there is the apt reference to the dawn which symbolizes the risen Christ. At evening prayer the Canticle of the Blessed Virgin Mary (the *Magnificat*) with its profound message of praise and thanksgiving is used. If a note of special dignity is desired at this point, some of the inspired and often inspiring settings from the past might be revived without any danger of reducing the assembly to a passive audience (see GILH 50).

At morning prayer the intercessions consecrate the coming day and its work to the Lord. Expressions of general and particular needs of the community as well as prayer for the living and the dead are contained in the petitions at evening prayer (GILH 51). The order of the rite is the same at morning prayer and evening prayer. The presider gives an introduction and announces the response; the assembly responds after each element before all say the Lord's Prayer together. A concluding prayer completes the hour.

The format of the intercessions or petitions is not rigidly fixed; neither is their content. Those proposed in the office may be used, added to, or replaced by others that are suitable. Indeed, it may be advisable for each community to include in this rite its own special intentions, those reflecting the reality of life together and thus making the prayers more personal and immediate. This does not imply change for the sake of change but recognizes that it is legitimate to vary the manner of liturgical celebration, perhaps using the texts given but also composing new texts which may be more relevant to local needs.

Some alternative ways of presenting the intercessions/petitions can now be considered:

- The assembly sings the response in answer to what one or two soloists have recited or sung. A variant here would be for a soloist to sing the first part of the intercession/petition, the second part to be sung by the choir and the response by the whole assembly, perhaps with the choir adding harmony.

- The response is changed during the recitation; one is used for the general intentions and another (simpler) one for any local or spontaneous requests. Another alternative might be to use an acclamation expressing the greatness of God in response to prayers of praise, whereas a supplicatory response would better suit prayers for assistance.

- A litany, for example, that of the Saints, may be substituted, or the short intercessions, which are litanic in form, may be used with the simple response sung by all.

- Many other possibilities exist, always respecting the norms laid down in numbers 51 and 179 to 193 of the General Instruction on the Liturgy of the Hours. These range from the spoken word over an instrumental or vocal ground, to a solo"cantillation" over an ostinato (e.g., the *Veni Sancte Spiritus* or the *Ubi Caritas* by Jacques Bertier from Taizé.)

If the intercessions/petitions have been sung, it seems right that the Our Father should also be sung, but never by the choir alone.

From this analysis of the structures of lauds and vespers, it is clear that everything could be sung except for the short readings which are to be spoken (GILH 268, 269). What, then, should be our priorities for singing or chanting? The numbers already referred to, together with number 277, indicate that hymns, psalms, canticles, and reponsories should be sung because of their intrinsically lyrical nature. To these are added responses to greetings and intercessions, antiphons, and other refrains.

In an attempt to answer the question, it is suggested that all who are concerned with the pastoral, liturgical and musical aspects of any celebration must have regard for the actual living community they seek to serve. In other words, one must recognize that there cannot be a single, universally valid answer because each case must take into account particular and variable local needs. A general guide to resolving this problem can be found in number 273 of the General Instruction on the Liturgy of the Hours.

> The principle of "progressive" solemnity therefore is one that recognizes several intermediate stages between singing the office in full and just reciting all the parts. Its application offers the possibility of a rich and pleasing variety. The criteria are the particular day or hour being celebrated, the character of the individual elements comprising the office, the size and composition of the community, as well as the number of singers available in the circumstances.

> With this increased range of variation, it is possible for the public praise of the Church to be sung more frequently than formerly and to be adapted in a variety of ways to different circumstances. There is also great hope that new ways and expressions of public worship may be found for our own age, as has clearly always happened in the life of the Church. (GILH 273)

We should also note that in the liturgies of the Mass and of the Hours the choice allowed can mean choosing not to sing but, where it is appropriate, to recite or to declaim. We must avoid making the prayer artificial or too complicated; at the same time we must preserve those moments of "holy silence."

Notes

1. See Constitution on the Sacred Liturgy, articles 9-10.

2. Italian Episcopal Conference, "Un servizio da prestare," in *Il rinnovamento liturgico in Italia* (1983) 9.

3. Piedmont Episcopal Conference, *I cori nella liturgia* (Leumann: LDC, 1988) note 3, 5-6.

4. C.M. Martini, "Attirerò tutti a me," in *Programmi pastorali diocesani 1980-1985* (Bologna: EDB, 1985²) I, 83.

3

Psychological Competence

Defining Psychological Competence and Its Necessity

A choir is composed of individuals who bring to the life of the group their own ways of thinking as well as their inner tensions, ideas, emotions, and aspirations. This makes for vitality and vivacity within the group, but it can also be a source of misunderstandings and clashes of temperaments which can be difficult to resolve. For this reason it is important for the success of the choir that the leader is able to communicate in a friendly and sympathetic manner with all the members of the group. It is not always easy to do this, especially when, perhaps, feelings of rivalry develop between singers. Again, it is difficult when criticism, which can be made in a positive or negative fashion, is necessary. A reproach for tardiness or lack of sufficient attention, when delivered in a tactless way, can do more harm than good and can even detract from the quality of the music-making.

It will be clear from the above that the choir director, even one well qualified liturgically and musically, may experience problems in group leadership and motivation. Some degree of psychological competence is clearly required.

This does not mean that the choir director must be a trained psychologist, but directing does demand some skills in coping with the many and various feelings, perceptions, intentions, memories, and understandings of the choir members. To be able to "manage" these disparate qualities in others, the director needs, before all else, self-confidence and a clear awareness of personal identity. Without these qualities it is difficult either to recognize the legitimate search for identity experienced by individual members or to handle the group dynamic.

Being responsible for directing others requires that a person be clear about his or her own values, about the priority those values have, and about the methods available to achieve them. For the Christian, the first criterion is not the importance of the music but the quality of the witness to Christ. If the link between the leadership role and the personal, spiritual commitment is not forged, then sooner or later there will be a crisis; it may be a musical/cultural crisis or even an identity crisis. Although the music itself may at times appear to offer a total experience, the music has to be set within a vision of life that implies values beyond and above the music. To build on being solely a musician or choir leader can lead to disappointment and frustration as soon as the first inevitable failures or difficulties arise. To overcome any inner doubts, psychology suggests a simple self-examination which asks what motivated the acceptance of the responsibility. The subject inquires, "Did I accept in order to please others (social compliance), to boost my own ego (personal identification), or out of a sense of vocation (internalization)?"

Social Compliance

- Accepting the position rather than running the risk of disappointing those in charge: the priest, the bishop, the liturgical commission, etc.

- Accepting because the choir members asked me, and I did not like to refuse them.

- Accepting because the rest of the choir seemed to think I was the best person available and expected me to take over when the previous choir director left.

In these examples the choir director accepted the responsibility in response to the requests of others, and yet did not necessarily possess the requisite qualities. An element of self-aggrandizement may also have motivated the acceptance.

Personal Identification

- I would like the position.
- I have what it takes.
- I get on well with most of the choir.
- Someone has to do the job and the parish would be grateful.
- I am the only one who is really competent so I have a right to the post.

Here the main motivation has been the self-interest of the person involved, who sees the position as offering self-fulfillment and status. Where the required expertise is present, this response is of a higher level than the first—leasing others. However, such a person may find difficulty in accepting criticism, may have problems in working with others and—when liturgical requirements clash with personal aesthetic judgments—may prove unable to appreciate the needs of the assembly.

Internalization

- I realize that I have certain gifts to place at the disposal of the community, and I am content to use them for as long as I am required.

- I am confident that I can achieve certain standards, but I am also aware that the music exists neither for its own sake nor for mine but must serve a worthier cause.

When the choice is made out of a sense of vocation or "calling" rather than in compliance with social expectations or personal satisfaction, then the motivation is of the highest order. Psychologically, there is a harmony between the already stated demands of the liturgy on a choir director and that inner integrity and faith which is also required.

Nevertheless, it is also right to recognize that the other motivations do not lack validity. To accept the position rather than to offend or disappoint is quite proper. A desire for personal satisfaction is not wrong. Acceptance out of a sense of vocation may have arisen from elements of the two other stages. What is important is that, whatever the level of motivation in the first place, a choir director should mature into a person who sees the service he or she gives as a vocation.

The first step toward the creation of a mature choir, from a psychological perspective, is the establishment of an identity. The second step involves an analysis of the motivations of the choir members.

Obviously we cannot question people on how well they understand their task. The choir director, however, has to succeed in a very different and subtle task; he or she needs to know, at a profound level, the members of the choir. This is not to judge them but to be able to draw them together in order to progress.

At the basis of any motivation there is a set of feelings, perceptions, and ideals which contribute to the creation of an "atmosphere" within the group. This "atmosphere" is important since it results from everyone sharing in the common task.

If we adapt what Alessandro Manenti has said about the family group to the concept of the choral group, we can suggest that a choir is not simply the sum of its members; if there are thirty members and one director, the choir is made up of not thirty-one but thirty-two components. The extra component is exactly this "atmosphere" which is a psychic element, produced by the sum of the forces involved, and a relational component created by the way these forces interact.

The reality of this "atmosphere" gives a living identity to the choir, an existence different from that of a simple group of individuals.[1] The degree to which this "atmosphere" exists in a state of equilibrium depends on the interactions of the different motivations.

If there is no effective internalization by either the singers or their director, the group—as a liturgical choir—will gradually lose its sense of purpose, and conflicts may arise. The internalization of motives creates the style of the choir. It informs the choir's ways of thinking, feeling, and interacting and this, in turn, makes the choir director aware of what courses should be followed within the group. Examination of the following scheme will suggest possible styles in the light of the interactions of the prevailing motivations.

CHOIR DIRECTOR (dominant motive) / CHOIR (dominant motive)	SOCIAL COMPLI-ANCE	PER-SONAL IDENTIFI-CATION	INTER-NALIZA-TION
SOCIAL COMPLIANCE	A	B	C
PERSONAL IDENTIFICATION	D	E	F
INTERNALIZATION	G	H	I

A - Most of the choir members, as well as the choir director, are merely being compliant. The result is chaos; there are no certainties; problems multiply; criticism is rife.

B - The director looks for personal public esteem and official recognition but fails to listen to the ideas of the choir members. They either become subdued and overawed by their self-seeking director, or they leave. This approach may be categorized as the director-dictator style.

C - In general, this is a transitional stage where one of the two components has reached the internalized motivation stage. A choir of this kind can improve when the director tries patiently to introduce values that go beyond the music itself but does so without exploiting, for his or her own self-aggrandizement, either the situation or the choir members.

The word "patiently" must be stressed because someone whose ultimate goal has been the pleasure of making music can hardly be expected to distinguish what, of popular music, is liturgically "good" or "functional."

Patience is required if internalization is to be achieved through musical and psychological growth. Our enthusiasm is required to motivate choristers but we must face reality; patience and sympathy are necessary if we are not to feel frustrated; so too is staying-power.

Compliant choir members will never directly criticize the manner or choices made by the director. To avoid misunderstandings, however, the director must aim for a dialogue with the choir; in a friendly manner the choir must be led to examine and analyze its role and work.

It may also be useful to have a "choir committee" whose members can contribute to choosing repertoire and can give a lead to the choir's activities. A useful tactic can be to involve in the committee's work choir members who like to gossip. "Patience" and "staying-power" are the watchwords for the choir director.

D - Another situation arises when a young and inexperienced musician, perhaps able to play a few guitar chords, is placed in charge of a group of young people whose motivation is immature. The leader may be shy or embarrassed, and consequently the group does not work well. Typical of this kind of choir is the choir that comes together only for special occasions like Midnight Mass, whereas ordinary Sundays are neglected. Either the group remains no more than a "Christmas Choir" or it moves on toward a more serious liturgical commitment.

E - Sometimes an apparently idyllic arrangement is upset by a quarrel; some slight criticism is seen as a personal insult. Often, when this happens, it is because the choir's focus is too exclusively musical, and its true liturgical importance is overlooked.

This kind of choir often has a high opinion of its own musical skills but has a poor opinion of others, less academically qualified or gifted. Too frequently such a choir has a poor sense of what is functionally or practically suitable; it regards the traditional, ancient music as the only music worthy of the liturgy. Even if the choir members are aware of the insights and instructions of the council, they are incapable of re-interpreting their role because doing so threatens their identity. In a word, their approach is narcissistic.

F - Akin to choir "C" described above is a choir where the leader has understood that the creation of music is a service to the assembly which wishes to celebrate, a choir whose gifts are dedicated to the common good. By good example and style the motives of the choir members are brought to maturity.

There is still criticism and a clash of ideas, but this arises from the leader being ahead of the choir in understanding the liturgical role. Yet again the leader must bring patience and staying power to the necessary dialogue—in Italian "ascolto attivo" or "active listening." The object must be to listen to the members and, when possible, to grant their wishes. At the same time, efforts must be made to bring home to the singers the importance of the assembly in which "Christ is really present" (see GIRM 7). They must be led to appreciate the beauty of the prayer and song of the whole community at worship.

G - Some groups exhibit a mature understanding of the liturgy, but are led by a person who has been coerced into the role. Where the members are willing and show understanding, the director can rapidly achieve a mature and more valid motivation for the work. Since the majority of the members have reached that degree of internalization described above, the prospects for such a choir are very good.

H - The stage following the situation of "E" requires the choir director to grow; failure to do so will result in the choir's collapse. The real needs of the members are liturgical, and the leader must recognize and conform to these needs.

I - This represents the highest ideal of a choir. The members are friends who create music together but who, in addition, strive to improve because they are motivated and stimulated by a set of values. These values stem from a human, a musical, and a religious understanding. The singers do not think of themselves as perfect as choir "E" does. Both choir director and members are mature and confident of their own identities. There is trust and communication between members and director, and this is based on a consciousness that singing in a truly liturgical choir is real service to others and an opportunity for personal spiritual growth. As one choir leader has said: "I feel deeply drawn to the members of the choir, and to some in particular, but I am always able to express my own ideas. I try to treat everyone alike, and I never take sides. Because I am ready to accept criticism, I have the courage to criticize when criticism is necessary."

Such a choir is a happy choir; no one feels threatened, no one is afraid of correction, no one feels upset or harshly judged when making a mistake. Such a choir is able to serve others.

In the scheme we have just examined, "motivation" has been used as a term to identify certain aspects of an approach to the work of a choir. We have considered social compliance, personal identification, and internalization. The general identity of a choir will depend upon the prevailing motivation.

It is necessary to remember that we can find all three kinds of motivation in varying degrees within one person or within one particular choir. The perfect choir may exist only as a theoretical ideal, but we must regard the ideal as our objective if we are to serve our communities better.

The Choir Director's Code of Honor

The way in which a choir director behaves has an crucial influence on the ability of the choir to serve either its corporate self or the community. At the first level, compliant choir members identify the director with themselves. To bolster their self-image, some choristers will note their director's every action, sometimes in a highly critical manner. In other cases a close collaboration and a mature understanding will transcend all else. This is why we have formulated a brief "code of honor" for the director.

- Do not take sides, but endeavor to establish friendly relationships with every member of the choir; address them clearly by name. This helps increase a sense of identity.

- Do not minimize your own competence. It is false modesty and undermines the confidence of the choir.

- Do not look to the choir to inflate your own importance, not even by the most subtle of means.

- Do not neglect any chorister who requires help to improve.

- Never withdraw any support you have given.

- Continue to develop your own knowledge and skills.

- Apply the rules of the group, apportioning blame when necessary; but do so tactfully and gently—remembering that members often come to rehearsals after a long day's work.

- Be generous with praise when it is earned, but be realistic and honest so that the members grow in their own understanding and appreciation of the work they do.

- Set attainable goals so that the choir members can see some point to their work. Begin rehearsing, say for Christmas, in plenty of time; perhaps work toward some extra-liturgical occasion or even a concert.

- Remember that tensions between some members can affect the morale of the whole group.

- Involve members in choosing repertoire.

- Delegate responsibility within the group and utilize the various abilities and skills available. One person may organize the venue, another may be in charge of the musical scores. Train one or two of the group to deputize for you. The choir does not have to depend upon one person alone to conduct, although you must set the values and ideals.

Note

1. See A. Dini Martino - A. Manenti, *Vivere in due o più aspetti sociologici e psicologici* (Rome: Paoline) 91-94.

4

Pedagogical Competence

Teaching a song is achieved by using either a theoretical or a practical approach. Differing levels of motivation and musical skill influence the task; the complexity of the music and the teaching skills of the choir director also play a part.

The Method: Psychological Considerations

First, the method must be chosen, and this depends on the nature of the individuals who make up the group and with whom a close relationship must be established. Whatever the musical and technical skills of the teacher, failure will result if this initial point is ignored.

According to some schools of psychology there are four necessary conditions to be fulfilled when we take as our starting point the people who constitute our choir.

- Respect for the opinions, ideas, and values of others and for their right to express them.
- Confidence in our own opinions, ideas, and values and in our right to express them without being upset by criticism. Confidence, also, in our authority and in our ability to make difficult decisions when required.
- The recognition that we need to be respected for our own specific qualities, skills, and motivation.
- Trust in our own professional talents and expertise which we have placed at the service of the community—in our particular circumstance, the Christian assembly.

Basically, without self-confidence the teacher cannot expect to create an atmosphere conducive to learning. A satisfactory musical level may be achieved but only with difficulty for all concerned, and enthusiasm will rapidly wane.

Just as important as self-confidence is a continual awareness that a liturgical choir is essentially a deeply committed group whose task is to pray as well as to sing.

The Method: Technical and Teaching Considerations

The first essential for the teacher is total familiarity with the song to be taught. Possible difficulties should have been anticipated: doubts or uncertainties will inevitably lead to a loss of confidence in the leader by the choir.

Learning

The first thing is to be familiar with each vocal line. Ability to read music makes it easier to pass from the score to the sound but, we must remember, many leaders of church choirs are unable to read musical notation. Recognition of this sad fact does not imply approval or acceptance of the situation, and it is difficult to imagine how a song can be really adequately taught when the ability to read is lacking. Relying on aural memory is risky;

leaders who are forced to do so should be encouraged to avail themselves of the many opportunities that exist for learning the rudiments of music.

Undesirable as lack of such a basic skill is, let us examine a possible way in which a piece may be taught by someone unable to read a score with ease.

Begin with a rhythmic approach which ignores the words, but do not adopt percussion, like hand-clapping, because this does not distinguish between long and short notes or rests. Rather, sing the rhythm to a single syllable like "lah" or "mo."

Teach the rhythm first, and when this has been firmly established add the melody. After each phrase or more difficult section check, with the aid of an instrument, that the correct pitch is being maintained.

Once rhythm, melody, and pitch have been learned, a rhythmic reading of the text can also help before you bring all the elements together.

For a leader with absolutely no reading skill, the only way to learn a piece is by imitating. Use a good recording, one that is faithful to the composer's and writer's wishes, since this will at least ensure uniformity of performance between communities. Never rely on the memory of a piece heard once during the course of a celebration.

Remember that rigid imitation is likely to be lifeless. Grasp the essential melodic line and omit the arrangement, however attractive. Even when learning by imitation, try to follow the score; the exercise will provide a first step toward acquiring the skill of reading and will also assist the memory when starting to teach the song.

Analysis and Preparation

After learning a song but before attempting to teach it, carefully analyze the elements of the piece; the "what" making up the kind of piece. Similarly consider the variables that will influence the performance: the "how," the "with whom," the "why," the "when," and the "where." Doing all this gives a chance to prepare not only on the musical level but also on the spiritual level necessary for liturgical music.

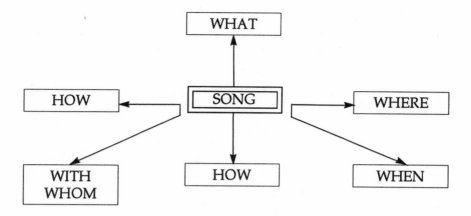

WHAT. Every song belongs to a particular genre and style in both words and music. An acclamation is clearly very different in both genre and style from a meditative chant or a devotional hymn. For a valid interpretation-performance-prayer we need to have a clear understanding of the piece; if we lack this understanding, do we not we run the risk of treating everything in a similar monotonous fashion?

Analyze carefully:

- Music: the tune, the rhythm, the harmony, the form; strophic, refrain, litany, hymn, motet, etc..
- Words: content, language, style, and again form.
- Relationship between music and text: each has its special effect, but do the two elements easily relate to each other? Does the music suit the text? Does the music have its origins in popular, rock, or classical music? What cultural impact will these origins have on the assembly, and will it help the celebration?

HOW. From the technical angle, how is the work to be presented? Should everyone sing, or should the voices alternate? Would a solo voice be best at any stage? This may be dictated by the form of the text and its content: is it the Lord who speaks, or is it a single person or a group of people? Is the song more suitable for a soloist, small group, full choir, or the congregation? Perhaps it calls for a judicious mixture of all these forces. Does the compatibility of text and music suggest any particular dynamics? Do we begin loudly or softly? How do we envisage the varying speeds or the intensity of feelings? How are we to highlight particular words or phrases? How about the speed, and where should there be any accelerando or rallentando? How do we deal with the difficult parts, and is there need to allocate them especially? How shall we arrange suitable and apt instrumentation?

WITH WHOM should we use the song? Will it suit a heterogeneous group such as a parish, or will it be better for a more homogeneous gathering according to age, culture, or level of faith? Is the assembly made up of sick people, young people, or children?

WHY this song in preference to any other? How does this song function? Does it fulfill a ritual requirement? As "some kinds of music are good or bad for dancing, relaxation, choral singing, private enjoyment, etc., so in the liturgy there are kinds of music that are good or not so good for various functions of the word—proclaiming, meditating, psalm-singing, praise, acclamation, dialogue, response etc.—and those that are useful or not so useful for different ritual moments: opening, processions, litanic supplication, and so on."[1]

Does it emphasize feelings, give cohesion to the group, continue a tradition? Does it fulfill a spiritual requirement? Does it assist the people who make up the assembly feel truly part of the celebration? "Taken in terms of faith, music for the believer becomes the *sacramentum* and the *mysterion* of the realities being celebrated."[2]

WHEN is the song to be sung? Is it for a special feast or for a Sunday? At what time of the day is it to be used? Will it be early in the celebration or later on? Remember that the quality of singing varies according to the time of day and the stage in the rite: voices need to warm up and are often better later in the day or in the event, but voices also tend to tire.

WHERE a piece is to be sung has its own influence on the choice we make. Singing in the open air creates its own problems. Places of pilgrimage, confraternities, or special groups often have their own music which works well in the context for which it was composed, but does this music function well outside this context?

From the many questions posed above about the music we select, it is clear that a very detailed preparation is necessary if we are to be efficient teachers. Simply to improvise our rehearsal shows a lack of respect for those we presume to teach; it shows how little regard we have for the content of liturgical music which is prayer.

The Rehearsal

We need to distinguish between two kinds of situations. The first is when we are rehearsing a choir that may range in ability from a small group of amateurs to a highly musically educated ensemble. The second is when we are faced with an assembly that is unlikely to be composed of trained musicians.

The Choir Rehearsal

When to rehearse always poses problems since no particular time will suit everyone. Nonetheless, it is wise to have a regular fixed time and day for rehearsal. If the time can be linked with some mid-week parish celebration, so much the better as this helps integrate the choir into the prayer life of the community which includes adults, young people, and children—all of whom may become involved in the choir.

Before starting to rehearse, the choir director must be thoroughly familiar with the material—this being the result of the preparation and analysis outlined above. The liturgical as well as the musical significance of any piece should be stressed. The content of the text and its function within the celebration should be explained.

A First Method of Teaching

When ready to teach a liturgical piece, always begin with the text. If a choir is to sing well, it must be aware of the importance of the words, and especially when the choir is singing the word of God. A possible procedure is the following:

- Urge everyone to read the text silently, encouraging them to ask questions about anything that is unclear or to offer suggestions. With a well-integrated group, this can be very fruitful.

- Recite the words in the rhythm of the piece in order to demonstrate the differences between the written and the spoken text.
- Briefly discuss, in the light of the previous analysis, how text and music inter-relate, and the kind of approach most likely to achieve a lively and prayerful performance.

- Introduce the melodic line, and consider whether it enhances or overwhelms the text.

- Take the choir through the song, phrase by musical phrase, pausing at the more difficult parts. When anything is to be repeated, explain why; this helps maintain attention and interest. With particularly difficult sections use some preliminary exercises on intervals and rhythms.

Now we can link the different parts, paying attention to details of performance and interpretation.

For a brief refrain or a short easy stanza, it is usually sufficient to repeat the whole section a number of times till everyone is familiar with it.

During any discussion listen sympathetically to all honest observations, however ill-informed they may be. Respect what the choir members may say and praise their enthusiasm; in this way both the individual and the communal sense of identity and self-esteem are strengthened, and this makes singing and praying together much easier.

A Second Method of Teaching

In this method we begin with the tune.

- The singers listen only to the melody, perhaps with a light accompaniment.

- Let them learn the tune; have them repeat it a number of times at different speeds but always rhythmically.

- Discuss the images or events suggested by the melody and draw together any general responses and ideas.

- Introduce the text; test how well the music reflects its ideas and note any relationships between the text and the emotions inspired by the music.

- Take the choir through the piece as in the last step of the First Method of Teaching.

A Third Method of Teaching

Listening to the whole piece provides yet another approach.

- The choir leader may demonstrate:
  — by singing through the whole piece;
  — by playing a record or tape-recording of the piece. This affords an opportunity to consider how appropriate the piece may be for the choir.

- Listen to any comments on what has been heard.

- Examine and explain the piece.

- Discuss how it might be successfully used and why it seems suitable.

- Learn the piece, again referring to the last section of the First Method of Teaching.

Teaching the Assembly

A liturgical choir's main responsibility is to involve the assembly in the music of worship. This means that the choir must be able to teach new music to the congregation and to lead it in a fuller participation in the celebration. The task of engaging the assembly more completely does not rest solely with the individual who actually guides the people, but it is shared with the choir.

How can the assembly be taught to play its part once compositions suitable to its needs have been chosen?

Usually their rehearsal has to occur just prior to the beginning of the celebration, although sometimes it is possible to make the practice part of the actual opening itself. Whatever the circumstances, the following ideas are helpful.

- If the choir is to sing in harmony, the people can be invited to sing the main tune but, as always, be sure you explain the reasons for the choice of music.

- Ask the assembly to repeat short phrases or sentences from the text until the complete work has been taught. Do not be discouraged by a poor response at first: the "musical memory" of the average congregation is limited.

- If the people are not accustomed to rehearsing, we cannot expect to teach anything new very quickly. It is probably best to introduce the people to rehearsals gently by asking them to sing, at first, only a short verse or refrain, one they can repeat easily. Praise their efforts, however shy or timid these might be.

For longer pieces (e.g., a new hymn) the choir can sing the piece at a previous celebration, and the people are invited to engage in active listening/praying so that they may become familiar with the music before attempting to sing it.

- Always insist upon accuracy and precision. Rhythmic and melodic mistakes destroy the integrity of the composition, and correcting what has been badly learned is extremely difficult.

If necessary, repeat accurately any part causing difficulty while explaining the reason for the repetition and offering an encouraging word or smile.

- If a well-chosen piece has been rehearsed before a celebration, it will not be difficult for the priest to establish a link between the piece and the liturgy, and the liturgical ideal of praying through song will be achieved.

The Method: Assessment and Evaluation

Any teaching method that does not incorporate some element of assessment and evaluation is incomplete. Without it we risk the assumption that our personal taste is infallible and our performance impeccable. As the choir's work follows the liturgical year, it is wise—at the beginning of the year and at set times during it—to stop, assess, and analyze what we are doing.

Assessing Needs

The life of a liturgical choir moves between two poles: the pastoral/liturgical and the musical/psychological. At the outset the musical director must consider two main aspects.

- What are the guiding principles of the pastoral plan?
- How best can the choir contribute and grow?

First, there must be liaison between everyone concerned with the pastoral and the liturgical program for the life of the community. Principles must be agreed upon and a plan drawn up—having the special times of Advent, Lent, and the Easter Season in mind.

Next, a realistic assessment of the choir's capabilities and its potential contribution to the community's needs must be made.

The year's plan, acknowledging the tensions between the two poles defined above, should take into account:

- What music in the current repertoire is of greatest value or merit and why?

- What new music may be introduced and why?

- What rites or times during the coming year may be best served by appropriate music? For example, the penitential rite during Lent may be highlighted by music, or the eucharistic prayer on Holy Thursday or Corpus Christi might be solemnly sung.

This prior assessment is equally important when arranging a particular celebration. The priest, the choir director, the liturgical group, and any others responsible for any part of the celebration must be clear about any special aspect of faith or practice that is to be stressed, the choice of readings, the theme of the homily, the nature of any symbols or gestures that are to be used (for example, the sign of peace).

We also need to be acutely conscious of the nature of the group that is assembling for the occasion. Is it homogeneous or heterogeneous, young or old? Whatever its composition, the members of the assembly are the prime reason for our work, and their requirements must form part of our considerations.

Evaluating the Work Done

In evaluating the contribution made by the choir and its leader to the worship of the community, we could ask the following questions.

- What kind of church community is shown by our liturgy?

- What would a visitor make of us?

- Do we project an atmosphere of joy?

- Does the assembly have an active role?

To evaluate the quality of the celebration, we should ask all who had been involved in the preparation and presentation to offer their reactions in the light of the actual experience.

- Was there a proper balance between the parts sung and the parts said?

- Were there too many or too few opportunities for music, and what reasons might there be for either case?

- How successfully did the music relate to what preceded or followed it?

- Did the choice of music and its performance help or hinder the prayers of the community?

If we are to achieve an honest and worthwhile assessment and evaluation, we—as leaders of choirs or musical groups—must consult with others in the community. We must consider every aspect of the task and, by means of assessment and evaluation, always seek to improve the quality of our offering.

Notes

1. Universa Laus Document (7.3) in *Music and Liturgy*, tr. Paul Inwood (Washington, D.C.: The Pastoral Press, 1992) 22.
2. Ibid. (7.4) 22-23.

5

From Analysis
to Final Product

Having examined in detail the song, the rehearsal, and the methods of teaching, we now turn to the manner of combining a piece's elements and variations in order to produce a valid performance from the choir, the congregation, and all who make the music—a performance suited, above all else, to the rite and to the circumstances of a particular assembly.

Not Only the Rhythm

Particular characteristics of any piece used in our celebration need to be brought out in order to reveal the selection's richness and to heighten understanding. The choir leader does this by

49

using gestures, and by gestures reminds the singers of subtleties of expression, details of interpretation, dynamics indicated in the score, etc. which have been discussed and rehearsed beforehand.

The most obvious purpose of these gestures is to bring about a vital and accurate musical presentation: precise intonation, correct rhythm and speed, clean endings. In addition, these gestures serve to indicate the nuances contained within the song. In spite of such a multiplicity of demands on them, the gestures must be clear, simple, and reduced to the very minimum necessary.

Inspiring Confidence

Our first task is to remain calm and relaxed in front of the singers. We know that we are prepared; we know that we are fully acquainted with the score; we know that we have analyzed the piece thoroughly. The musicians are well rehearsed, and we have made the piece our own.

Confidence is vital. If we are not confident, every gesture will betray our nervousness, and the psychological effect of timidity or uncertainty is total confusion.

Good, clear conducting stems from our own inner equilibrium and proper motivation.

Conducting for Real

This equilibrium, arising from our mental outlook, brings about a relaxation of the shoulders, upper arms, forearms, wrists, hands, and fingers. We need to be conscious of each of these elements because they are the means whereby we direct the choir; and yet, above all, our state of mind dictates the spirit of the performance.

To indicate a *pianissimo*, use just the fingers; but for *piano* the hand is required; using the forearm indicates *mezzo-forte*, whereas moving the whole arm demands a *forte*.

With experience comes the realization that other gestures can convey more subtle indications which implore, calm, encourage, or invite prayerfulness. Light or gentle tone is evoked by relaxed and soothing use of the fingers and hands, whereas a strongly rhythmic reaction is brought about by using stiff fingers and exploiting the movement of the wrist while the hand is closed and the forefinger points.

Let us look at four simple gestures that seek particular responses:

- the hand that drives on or holds moves from right to left;
- movement from left to right is welcoming, inviting;
- moving the hand upward calls for a sustained or increased intensity;
- a downward movement softens, calms, and approves.

All the gestures serve two purposes: rhythm and expression. The rhythm must be maintained and the tempo indicated: this is done by the right hand. The expressive and interpretive aspects are conveyed by the left hand. This is why both hands and arms must work, but they do not perform similar gestures. Normally for one hand to duplicate the actions of the other is pointless except, perhaps, when directing a very large assembly.

How to Begin

A poor start is inevitable if the initial gesture is not clear. Three stages are required, and these can be characterized as:
- Attention;
- Preparation;
- Start.

Attention. The first gesture has to attract and focus the attention of the choir. Begin by taking an overall look at all the musicians; then raise the hands a little above shoulder height, but do not cover the face. Hold this position for a few seconds to ensure that everyone is watching.

Preparation. At this stage open the hand with the palm down and prepare to give the pitch, if necessary, before indicating the initial tempo. Give some sign of when to take the important preparatory breath so that firm intonation is ensured.

This "breathe" gesture needs to lead from the act of inhaling to the production of the first note. Generally a gentle, upward movement is sufficient, though occasionally something different is better, but this will be described later.

This Preparation stage precedes the Start so it must be placed in the context of the tempo and rhythm. For example, if a piece is to begin on the third beat of a bar, the preparatory gestures must be made during the second beat.

Start. This action falls on the actual starting note. If the "Preparation" has been successful, this third stage is almost a formality; but before we go on to examine the various methods of attack, let us remember the vital rule—to avoid all unnecessary gestures which can divert rather than direct attention.

Setting and Maintaining the Time

Setting and maintaining the tempo requires different patterns of movement according to the various time signatures (2/2, 3/4, common time) and the placing of the initial note within the bar. Each time signature has its own precise pattern of movement, and improvisation is not advisable unless one has had much experience. The following diagrams for the main time signatures will help us understand the usual gestures employed.

A. Two Beats to the Measure: 2/4, 2/2, 6/8

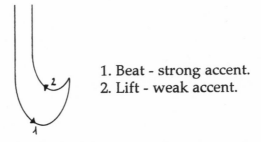

1. Beat - strong accent.
2. Lift - weak accent.

The first beat must bounce back, clear and precise. A strong accent implies a marked gesture whereas a weak accent requires a more delicate but never a vague movement. Let us examine the different ways in which pieces in duple (two) time may begin.

A-1. Two Beats: Starting on the First Beat

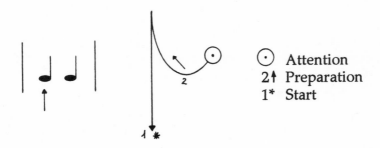

⊙ Attention
2↑ Preparation
1* Start

Example:

Joy to the World

Joy to the world! the Lord is come; Let earth re - ceive her King;

Text: Psalm 98; Isaac Watts, 1674-1748. Music: George F. Handel, 1685-1759, in T. Hawkes' *Collection of Tunes*, 1833.

The "attention" gesture, with stiff arm and forearm, is placed toward the right at about chest height. The preparatory move is made by raising the hand on the second beat prior to the "start" being indicated by bringing the hand down firmly and exactly.

A-2. Two Beats: Starting on the Second Beat

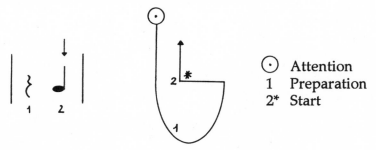

⊙ Attention
1 Preparation
2* Start

Example:

When We Eat This Bread

When we eat this bread and we drink this cup,

we pro - claim your death un - til you come.

Here the most difficult moment is that of preparation. The hand must descend from the "attention" point to the first beat and then rise. The "attention" point is placed head-high; and the following, preparatory movement is indicated by the open hand falling and rising; a gesture which, of itself, suggests taking breath.

A-3. Two Beats: Starting on the Second Half of the First Beat

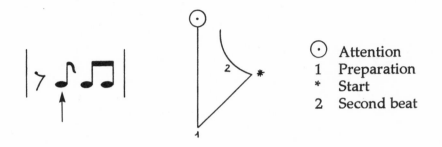

☉ Attention
1 Preparation
* Start
2 Second beat

Example:

O Bless the Lord

O bless the Lord,___ the God of our sal - va - tion,

Rock___ of strength and a ref - uge sure!

Again the "attention" point must be high, and the movement though the "preparation" to "start" passes the point of the first beat gently and with the hand open until the "start" is reached.

A-4. Two Beats: Starting on the Second Half of the Second Beat

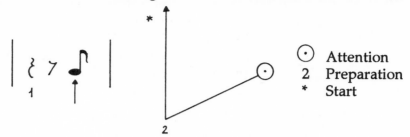

⊙ Attention
2 Preparation
* Start

Example:

The Bread That We Break

The bread__ that we break is a shar-ing in Christ's bod - y; the

cup__ that we bless a com - mun - ion in his blood.

Here the "attention" point is moved to the right, and the preparatory gesture is upwards towards the "start." It may appear strange to start on an upward beat like this, but it serves to mark the stress on the following strong accent.

B. Three Beats in the Measure: 3/2, 3/4, 3/8.

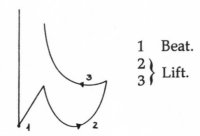

1 Beat.
2 } Lift.
3 }

It is important here to indicate clearly the difference between the first, strong beat, and the following two weaker beats. The more we bring out the difference, the more the piece acquires a waving, dancing motion with one strong stress and two weaker stresses. With regard to the gestures, let us again look at the different examples we might experience.

B-1. Three Beats: Beginning on the First Beat

Example:

Alleluia Sing To Jesus

Al - le - lu - ia! Sing to Je - sus! His the scep - ter, his___ the throne.

Text: Revelation 5:9; William Dix, 1837-1898, and others. Music: Rowland H. Prichard, 1811-1887.

The attack has the same characteristics demonstrated above for conducting two in the bar.

B-2. Three Beats: Starting on the Second Beat

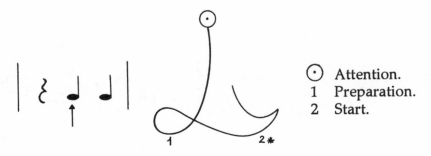

⊙ Attention.
1 Preparation.
2 Start.

Example:

The Strife Is O'er

Text: *Finita iam sunt praelia,* Latin 12th century, tr. by Francis Pott, 1832-1909, alt. Music: Giovanni da Palestrina, 1525-1594, adapted by W.H. Monk, 1823-1889.

This is a rather difficult start. "Attention" is at the top, and the "Preparation" when the forearm falls with the hand open; the "Start" comes on the second movement.

B-3. Three Beats: Starting on the Third Beat

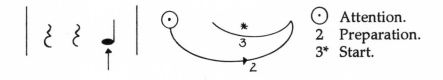

Example:

Amazing Grace

Text: John Newton, 1725-1807. Music: *Virginia Harmony,* 1831.

B-4. Three Beats: Starting on the Second Half of the First Beat

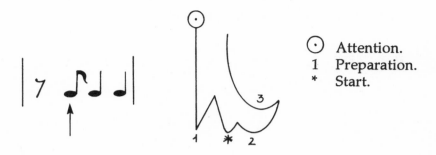

- ⊙ Attention.
- 1 Preparation.
- * Start.

Rarely encountered but given here for completeness, the preparatory gesture moves to the left after a slight raising of the hand.

B-5. Three Beats: Starting on the Second Half of the Second Beat

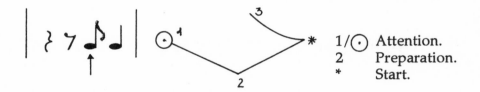

- 1/⊙ Attention.
- 2 Preparation.
- * Start.

Again a rare occurrence. Uniquely we move the hand from left to right in a single gesture at the end of which we have our "Start."

B-6. Three Beats: Starting on the Second Half of the Third Beat

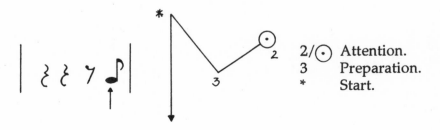

- 2/⊙ Attention.
- 3 Preparation.
- * Start.

Example:

O Blessed Are Those

O blessed are those who fear the Lord and walk in his ways, O

blessed are those who fear the Lord and walk in his ways.

"Attention" is placed up and to the right; "Preparation" takes place through the third beat to the "Start" at the top.

C. Four Beats in the Measure: C, 4/4, 4/2, 4/8.

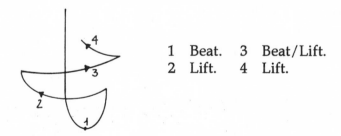

1   Beat.   3   Beat/Lift.
2   Lift.   4   Lift.

In quadruple (four) time it is necessary to stress the first and the third beats in order to emphasize the rhythmic division into 2+2 beats. A strong first beat is followed by a weak second beat, a semi-stressed third beat, and finally a weaker fourth beat. Again, let us consider the various methods of attack.

C-1. Four Beats: Starting on the First Beat

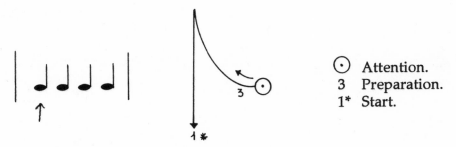

⊙ Attention.
3 Preparation.
1* Start.

Example:

Crown Him with Many Crowns

Crown him with man - y crowns, The Lamb up - on his throne; All

king-doms of the earth re - sound In praise of him a - lone.

Text: Matthew Bridges, 1800-1894. Music: George Elvey, 1816-1893.

This measure on the first beat is introduced in a similar manner to the introductions for 2 or 3 beats in the bar.

C-2: Four Beats: Starting on the Second Beat

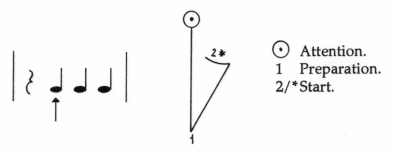

⊙ Attention.
1 Preparation.
2/*Start.

(The preparatory movement should be made lightly.)

Example:

Behold the Glory of God

"Preparation" takes place during the first beat. Do not round the gesture nor open the hand; doing so may confuse the singers and lead to someone mistaking the preparatory movement as the indication to begin.

C-3. Four Beats: Starting on the Third Beat

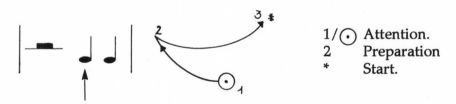

1/⊙ Attention.
2   Preparation
*   Start.

Example:

Praise God from Whom All Blessing Flow
(Old Hundredth)

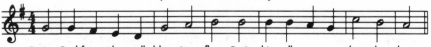

Text: Thomas Ken, 1637-1711. Music: Louis Bourgeois, c. 1510-1561.

Since we can think of quadruple (four) time as being two measures of two beats, we can start on the third beat as if it were the first beat in a measure of two.

C-4. Four Beats: Starting on the Fourth Beat

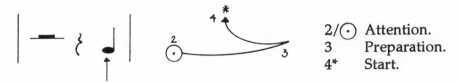

2/⊙	Attention.
3	Preparation.
4*	Start.

Example:

O Sacred Head

O   Sa-cred Head, sur-round-ed   By   crown of pierc-ing   thorn!   O

bleed-ing Head, so   wound-ed,   Re-viled and   put___   to   scorn!

Text: ascr. to Bernard of Clairvaux, 1091-1153, alt. Music: Hans Leo Hassler, 1564-1612.

Here we can indicate the start as if it were the second beat in a measure of two.

C-5. Four Beats: Starting on the Second Half of the First Beat

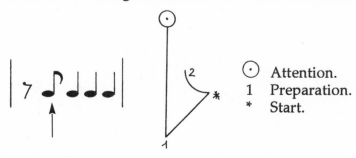

⊙	Attention.
1	Preparation.
*	Start.

Example:

I Will Not Die

I will not die be-fore I've lived to see that land;

firm as the earth, God's own prom-ise.___

This is analogous to the second case in duple (two) time (see A-2 above).

C-6. Four Beats: Starting on the Second Half of the Second Beat

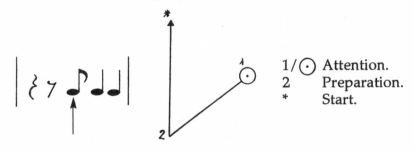

1/⊙ Attention.
2   Preparation.
*   Start.

Example:

Earthen Vessels

We hold a treas-ure,___ not made of gold,

in earth-en ves-sels, wealth un-told,___

See the fourth case in duple (two) time (A-4)

C-7. Four Beats: Starting on the Second Half of the Third Beat

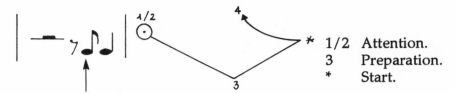

The start is indicated in the same way as it is in Case 5 in triple (three) time (see B-5 above).

C-8. Four Beats: Starting on the Second Half of the Fourth Beat

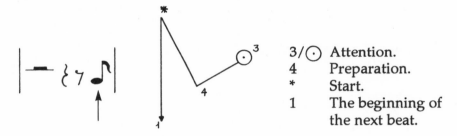

Example:

How Can I Keep From Singing

My life flows on in end-less song;— a-bove earth's

lam - en - ta - tion._____ I hear the real though

This is rather similar to the fourth case in duple (two) time (see A-4) or the sixth case in triple (three) time (see B-6).

D. One Beat in the Measure - 3/8, or
Two Beats in the Measure - 6/8.

When we consider a rhythm in compound time, such as 3/8 or 6/8, it is useful to regard the eighth note as the base unit of our gesture. For 3/8 is sufficient to refer back to how to conduct three beats in the bar. With 6/8, however, it may be better to allow the movement to flow through the second and third and the fifth and sixth eighth notes in order to avoid making too many, perhaps heavy, gestures.

In a particularly slow moving piece it may be useful to divide the bar into more beats in order to be more precise with the stresses. To do this it is sufficient to repeat, in a reduced form, each single gesture of the beat. This can also be done to achieve a *rallentando* (reduction in speed) or a particular counter rhythm.

The sub-divisions of a compound duple rhythm: 6/8.

The sub-divisions of a compound triple rhythm: 9/8.

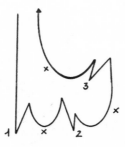

The sub-divisions of a compound quadruple rhythm: 12/8.

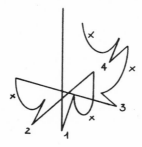

But beware! If this last, complicated gesture is unnecessary or is not completely understood by choir leader and choir, do not attempt it; it can cause chaos.

E. Five Beats in the Measure

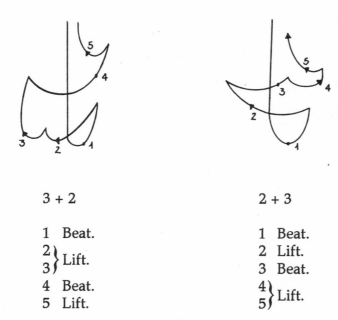

3 + 2	2 + 3
1 Beat.	1 Beat.
2⎫ Lift.	2 Lift.
3⎭	3 Beat.
4 Beat.	4⎫ Lift.
5 Lift.	5⎭

There are two ways of dividing the five beats: into three and two (with the accents on the first and the fourth beats) or into two and three (with the accents on the first and the third beats). The following example demonstrates the first of these alternatives.

Example:

Sing of the Lord's Goodness

Sing of the Lord's good - ness, Fa - ther of all wis - dom,

come to him and bless his name. _____

F. Six Beats in the Measure

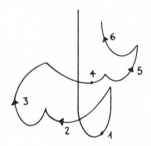

Generally this rhythmic pattern is regarded as being in compound time, and the strong accent is placed on the first beat and the weaker accent on the fourth beat.

Example:

We Shall Draw Water (503).

How to Finish

So far we have looked at starting and directing the course of a piece of music, now we turn to how to finish it properly. Again we have to prepare and to do this we must ensure, by a quick glance followed by an agreed gesture such as a clear lift of the forefinger, that we have the attention of the musicians.

The preparatory signal for the conclusion could be a circular movement leading to a clear downward gesture which indicates "stop." These are rather formal directions, but they are in keeping with the precise lead given throughout the whole performance. With a trained choir it may be sufficient to give only a glance. If the final note is a climax, however, the gesture must sustain the intensity and, even more importantly, the tone. This can be invited by keeping the hand stiff, a little forward and the palm uppermost.

But the end of the song is not the end of the matter. Try not to cause distraction with rustling of copies, with comments or fits of coughing especially when a work has been sung in the context of a celebration.

What has been said above about conducting is not a definitive exposition nor is it the only way. It is one tried and tested method. Through experience the choir director will develop a personal style. What must always be remembered is that superficiality will not bring good results. Conducting everything in exactly the same way, under the pretense of using a simple or straight-forward manner, may prove to be synonymous with incompetence.

To strive for a musical, rhythmically precise, and artistically satisfying interpretation is a duty imposed by the music, the musicians, and the circumstances of the celebration.

Conducting the Assembly

The assembly needs its own special guidance, and sometimes the choir director acquires such an added responsibility. When this happens, it is necessary to treat the assembly and the choir differently. Gestures, understood by experienced singers in the choir, may well be too complicated for the assembly to understand or follow; too precise or elaborate direction of the assembly may distract from, rather than foster, their prayerful participation in the music of the liturgy. The simplest approach is to indicate, by appropriate movements of hand and arm, every pulse or note of the piece. This should be done in a direct, natural, and rather instinctive way.

The arm should move up and down, and the exact moment of the beat occurs when the hand reaches the lowest point before it rebounds. Generally speaking, a large and crowded assembly is best served by using vertical gestures. For a smaller assembly, however, horizontal movements from left to right and vice versa may prove to be more suitable. If we use vertical movements, a downward direction indicates each individual beat whereas an upward move is neutral and simply preparatory for the next beat.

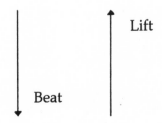

If we use the horizontal method bringing the arm across the body serves the same purpose as the Lift in the vertical pattern: it attracts attention and concentration. The beat occurs at the point when the hand is at its furthest from the body. The effect is soothing and restful.

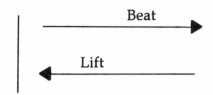

The most elegant gesture for indicating each beat of the rhythm is a combination of the horizontal and the vertical.

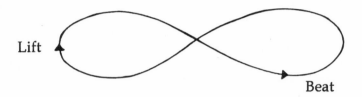

However the vertical pattern is the more precise in showing, as it does, the exact moment of the beat when the gesture reaches its lowest point. It does not matter how many notes the particular measure may have; what is important is that the individual notes be indicated rhythmically and clearly.

This method of conducting is especially suitable for songs in which the time signatures alternate or where there is no well defined time structure as, for example, in tunes like "Rendez à Dieu."

Example:

Conducting according to each beat or pulse does not distinguish between strong and weak accents. In pieces requiring some movement, a single, strong gesture for each note is best. In a more leisurely paced song it may be helpful to give two gestures for each beat, thereby suggesting the extra length of the notes. Using this technique places greater emphasis on the rhythmic aspects of the music rather than on its interpretation, but we cannot ignore the content of the song if we want the performance to fulfill its proper purpose in the celebration.

The character of a song may suggest a particularly strong gesture or, perhaps, something more restrained and gentle. In any case, useless gestures must be avoided. If the assembly has been given a clear "start," it can often be left to continue on its own. If it has taken matters into its own hands then the best course is to refrain from any further attempts at direction.

Indicating the Melody

One of the choir's main functions is to support the assembly. The choir must not only allow the assembly to sing but must, above all, assist in teaching unfamiliar music. In developing this choir/assembly partnership, help is often needed in learning new tunes. To do this, it is useful to employ gestures that suggest the musical intervals to be sung. This technique might be called "melodic direction" and consists of moving the hand up or down the vertical line in order to show a descending or ascending interval. For example:

1. The vertical, downward movement of the hand in a straight line indicates a close descending interval (la-sol).

2.   A similar movement in a curved line shows a wider descending interval (sol-mi, sol-re).

3.   An ascending vertical movement in a straight line will show a close ascending interval (mi-fah).

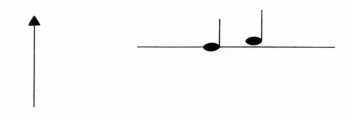

4.   A similar movement in a curved line shows indicates a wider ascending interval.

5.   To indicate a repeated note, it will suffice to move the hand in a horizontal line.

Let us look at a concrete example.

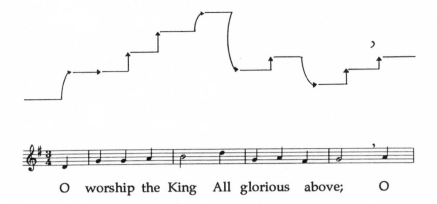

O   worship   the   King   All   glorious   above;   O

As far as the movements are concerned, this technique is not difficult. It presents a slight problem with regard to the rhythm, since only the pitch of the notes—not their duration or expressive quality—can been shown before they are actually sung. But the difficulties encountered in directing the music of the liturgy are no excuse for giving up; we should constantly be looking to further our study and to find solutions.

Directing the Chant

"What ever has happened to the beautiful Gregorian chant and the old, polyphonic music?"

"Why don"t we still sing the lovely Gregorian melodies with their haunting organ accompaniments?"

Many of us have faced such questions and sooner or later have had to answer them although they betray a lack of knowledge and of understanding. First, the ancient chants and polyphony are still used, though not as widely as formerly. Second, their continued use is encouraged by many official documents, e.g., *Sacrosanctum Concilium* (art. 116) which endorses Gregorian chant "as specially suited to the Roman liturgy" or the General Instruction on the Liturgy of the Hours (no. 274) which says that in "celebrations sung in Latin, Gregorian chant, as proper to the Roman liturgy, should have pride of place, all other things being equal."

Gregorian Chant: A Brief Historical Background

Gregorian chant owes its name to St. Gregory the Great, pope from 590 to 604. Gregory had been a Benedictine monk early in his life and would have been familiar with monastic music. When he became pope, he reformed the Roman *schola cantorum*, the official seminary for church musicians, arranging their repertoire of chants and enlarging it with many new ones inspired by a Christian spirituality. He also sought to extend his reform to all Europe.

Musically the original Gregorian chant was based on very simple tunes, one note allotted to each syllable of the text. The only variation was for the final words which might be enriched with extra notes. This simple form of melody was called "psalmody" and implied a dialogue either between the priest and the congregation when it was described as "responsorial," or between two groups of singers when the term "antiphonal" was used.

Beginning as pure vocal monody, chant used no instrumental accompaniment. The organ, with its non-Christian associations, was a late introduction into the liturgy and, strictly speaking, the use of the organ or any instrumental accompaniment for the early chant or polyphonic music is not authentic. "Haunting accompaniments" are really only acceptable if the voices are such that they need some support—ideally accompaniments should not be used.

Rhythmically, Gregorian chant is free moving and not metrical. It has a precise but unfettered rhythm which is linked to the stresses of the Latin words and not to any superimposed rhythmic pattern.

Gradually the rule requiring only one note for each syllable lost its importance, and single syllables acquired many notes; this gave rise to the more ornate or semi-ornate, melismatic forms of chant. Basic Gregorian melodies were retained, but the creativity of the musicians added to their simple structures. At first the music was sufficient for the texts, but as it became more elaborate, it became more difficult to remember; as an aid to the musical memory more words were inserted into the original text. These additions became known as "tropes," a word which may derive from the Provencal "*trobar*" meaning "to compose" or from the late Latin "*tropare*," i.e., "to sing." For instance, the creative musician would take the music of an Alleluia *jubilus* and add appropriate words which, in time, assumed independent status and came to be known as "sequences."

Whereas the word "Gregorian" describes a well-defined musical style with certain distinctive features, it must be remembered that the style developed and evolved over a long period. In order to understand this last statement more clearly, let us consider what we mean today by "Gregorian chant."

• The classical Gregorian syllabic style which is associated with passages for the liturgy of the hours and for the simpler chants used for what was called the Common of the Mass—Kyrie, Gloria, Credo, etc. These are the more accessible styles which have been especially commended as suitable for general use by some post-conciliar documents.

• The ornate or semi-ornate, melismatic Gregorian music derived from a time up to the eleventh century and which is generally typical of settings for the Proper of the Mass—introts, graduals, offertories, etc,—and for the responsories and antiphons for the liturgy of the hours. These are in a highly sophisticated style which requires, realistically, trained and experienced singers for their performance.

• The chant that has been devised since the actual classical Gregorian period, but employs the early style and spirituality. In this category we find works that imitate the original forms but have been created since the eleventh century right up to our own times. Examples include the seventeenth-century Credo III to settings devised in our own time for the eucharistic proclamations of the mystery of faith. These later chants have, naturally, been influenced by different cultures and may vary from the classical chant in the manner of their interpretation. This last point is expanded below.

From this short historical survey we can draw some conclusions:

• The more ornate chants may be unsuitable for our ordinary parish liturgies. Although regarded as the ideal, they are too difficult for performance by untrained singers. Their format and style may be completely alien to an assembly, and nowadays we have to ask of any music for the liturgy, does it truly expresses the spirituality of the group that is to use it? To employ a repertoire simply to gratify feelings of nostalgia or for the sentiments it may engender is culturally dishonest and liturgically unacceptable.

• The simpler, "syllabic" Gregorian style may be used with success only if the close relationship of words to music is fully realized. The melody is not distinct from the text but must arise naturally from the stresses and quantities of each Latin syllable.

As we know, the movement is free but never haphazard, always dependent upon the rhythm of the words. It is vital, consequently, that the choir director has a clear grasp of the underlying rhythm and flow of the Latin text. Without such knowledge and understanding of the Latin, it is unwise to attempt any performance of this specialized music.

• The later music, derived from the Gregorian and sometimes described as "corrupt," includes such pieces as the *Corde Natus* ("Of the Father's Love Begotten") or the Easter hymn *O Filii et Filiae* ("Ye Sons and Daughters") which sometimes appear in a strictly metrical form which preserves the melodies intact but destroys the rhythm. Such adaptations, which use the local language instead of the Latin, may have a certain limited but justified use, although the original, free-flowing melody is to be preferred.

A Method of Conducting Gregorian Music

Ideally, since conducting Gregorian chant is far from easy, long training with a competent teacher is desirable; also desirable is a clear understanding of Gregorian notation with its use of the four line stave. Unfortunately such instruction is not often readily available nor is the knowledge widespread. What follows is an attempt to provide some insight into a technique that can be employed, and in the course of which we have used the more familiar but less precise or subtle five line stave.

In light of what has been said above about the close relationship between text and music, a method must be devised that recognizes this link. This may, rather clumsily, be described as a "textual/melodic" direction because it arises from an analysis of both elements.

By way of example, let us look at the first stanza of the hymn *Veni Creator Spiritus*, a text by Rabanus Maurus (766-856) with music from the ninth century or even earlier and which is mainly syllabic and only slightly semi-ornate.

The text must be learned, its message absorbed, and its verbal structure understood.

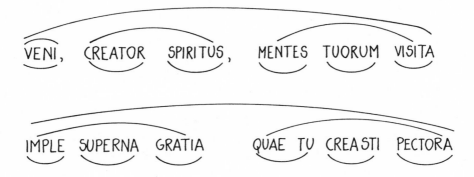

From this diagram the shape, pattern, and balance of the stanza can be seen; what might be called its "global unity."

A translation of the text would be:

> Come, Creator Spirit,
> Visit the minds which are yours,
> Fill with highest grace
> The breasts which you have created.

Pectora, literally "breasts," could be understood as "hearts" or even as "souls." *Creare* in late Latin can mean "to make grow" with the idea of a continuing process.

The main verbs, *veni - visita - imple*, are imperatives with optative qualities that carry overtones of respect, faith, and hope. The text is at once invocation and contemplation—a personal dialogue with the God to whom we give the first place in our prayer and our song.

Any gesture must convey the continuity from *Veni* right through to *pectora* without breaking up either the sentence or the thought.

Below the text, slurs indicate the individual elements of the verse; above it two lines of slurs show the sections and sub-sections. The longer slurs above the two lines of the hymn indicate the two main sections of the stanza; the first ending with *visita*. After that word there is a colon allowing time for a gentle breath which must not disturb the global unity of which we spoke.

Each subsection of these two main sections is, in turn, marked by the shorter slurs above the words. The first of the main sections has three shorter slurs, the first over *Veni*; the second main section has only two. All these sections have to be conducted in a manner allowing for the easy flow of the underlying dynamic of the text.

Each word is an essential part of the text; each has its own integral qualities of stress and quantity which must be observed. The text has to be conducted as an entity; we have to avoid any arbitrary emphasis on any particular word but give due recognition to its qualities. An actual attempt at performance may demonstrate which words and, above all, which ideas need to be underlined by directional gestures.

The melody, in the Gregorian manner, has to coincide closely with the text. Let us now examine the tune itself in relation to the words but without worrying yet about any gestures that may be required.

Here the sections are marked by quarter bars and half bars, and the appropriate syllables are marked with their accents. These must be observed to create a tuneful dynamism and an organic flow.

We can see how each accent (arsis) moves towards a point of rest (thesis). Our gestures must convey these characteristics in order to maintain melodic continuity.

This explanation may appear to be too pedantic, but the nature of Gregorian chant requires this detailed examination. The choir director has to be aware of these implications to be capable of transforming the music into prayer.

From Text/Music to Conducting

Thus far we have paid no attention to the kind of gestures best suited for conducting Gregorian chant. From the foregoing examination of the text and the music, some practical considerations become clear. Every piece of Gregorian music makes its own individual demands. The gestures need to arise from the movement of the piece itself and in an almost spontaneous fashion rather than from attempting a strict beat which is alien to the chant. The smoother the gestures are, the more likely they will correspond to the demands of the piece. This is akin to the methods described above in Conducting the Assembly, where the pulse or rhythm of the words become the basis of the direction given. As before, any gestures must be tailored to match the skills and competencies of the choir and the assembly.

Directing Psalmody

The suggestions made about using the pulse of the words as the basis for directing Gregorian chant stem from the close relationship, which is one of chant's main characteristics, between text and music. For similar reasons this technique may be used, with only slight adaptation, for directing psalmody, provided one is aware of the differences between psalms and, for example, songs.

For a fuller definition of the characteristics of the psalms and the various styles of performance, see Chapter 2.

Conclusion

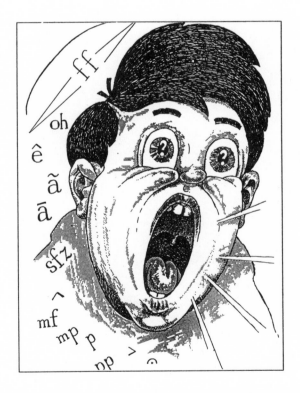

"The demands made by Christian ritual music spring from the ultimate goal of this music, which is to manifest and make real a new humanity in the risen Jesus Christ. Its truth, worth, and grace are not only measured by its capacity to arouse active participation, nor by its aesthetic cultural value, nor its long history of acceptance in the church, nor by its popular success, but because it allows believers to cry out the *Kyrie eleisons* of the oppressed, to sing the *Alleluias* of those restored to life, and to uphold the *Maranatha* of the faithful in the hope of the coming of the Kingdom." (Universa Laus Document, para 10.1)

All the liturgical, cultural and personal development of any director of liturgical music must be guided along this path.

Appendix

Appendix 1

The Singing Voice

"I can't sing. I'm always out of tune. Ever since I was a
child everyone has said it is awful to hear to me trying."

Many people believe that they are unable to sing simply
because they have never sung. But is the ability to sing in tune
really a talent given to only a few?

Nature has, in fact, given a musical instrument to each one of
us. Difficulties arise because so many of us fail to use this gift to
its fullest extent. Everyone possesses a voice and, with it, an in-
built faculty for speech and song. Speaking and singing are
natural phenomena; they are as fundamental as breathing or
sleeping.

If, as we assert, singing is as instinctive as speaking, sleeping, breathing, and thinking, then singing—like any other ability—can be developed. Look at the faculty of speech; if a child never hears a word uttered, is never spoken to or if its every effort is greeted with mockery, that child will never learn to speak. In the same way, the child who does not hear singing or is laughed at when trying to sing will never feel drawn toward singing and will always regard singing as something to be avoided. Never having practiced singing or, having tried and been derided, leads many people to conclude that they cannot sing.

Often a belief that one cannot sing in tune stems from a lack of knowledge about the voice and its capabilities and from a lack of practice in ways to control the production of sound. It is possible to remedy such a situation if there is a strong motivation. These outlines of how to sing can provide a useful introduction to any person who desires to try either solo or choral singing.

Developing a Good Singing Voice: Is It Possible?

The most important things are wanting to sing and being ready to work toward that end. The goal is not to imitate some abstract idea of a "perfect voice" but to train and develop the uniquely personal voices we already possess.

How the Voice Works

In order to sing well it is helpful to know something of what happens when we use our voices for either speech or song.

The instrument through which we speak or sing comprises the mouth, the pharynx, the larynx, the trachea, the bronchi, and the lungs. It works like a wind instrument through the twin actions of breathing air in and then breathing it out under pressure.

• The **larynx** is made up of muscular cartilage which forms a cavity. In this cavity the air encounters two vocal cords which cause the air to vibrate. The subconscious variation of the tension of these cords produces the particular notes required. Sounds, created by the air passing over the vocal cords, are enlarged and enhanced by the resonating cavities within the body.

• The **thoracic cavity**, within the chest, strengthens and enhances the deeper sounds of what is sometimes called the "chest register" or "chest voice."

- The **oral cavities** reinforce the sounds in the middle range of the voice.

- The **nasal cavities**, or sinuses, influence the quality of the higher sounds.

Oral and nasal cavities are situated in the head, and the sounds most affected by them are often referred to as the "head register" or "head voice."

Clearly, all these cavities or resonators effect the quality or timbre of the voice. Since we all possess unique and varied physical characteristics, the timbre of each voice will—quite naturally—be different. We should not feel frustrated that we are unable to produce a particular kind of voice, nor should we try to imitate any one voice or other; our task is to educate our own individual voices.

Is the production of sound solely instinctive or can we, by making more effective use of our breath—the power source for singing—improve the timbre of the voice even though we cannot alter the physique from which it originates? The answer is that we can, and—since the lungs are the first essential part of the instrument—the initial step is to learn how to control our breathing.

Learning to Breathe

Correct breathing is important not only for singing but even for our ordinary daily living. The better we breath, the better our quality of life. For instance, correct, controlled breathing in a stressful or difficult situation can help to confront the problem in a quieter, more relaxed frame of mind, and this is often the first step toward a solution.

There are two distinct methods of breathing. One uses movement of the chest and shoulders to expand the thoracic cavity and thus draw air into the lungs (thoracic or clavicular breathing). The other employs the diaphragm to achieve the same results (diaphragmatic or abdominal breathing). The consequences of each method are quite different.

When we try to inhale by lifting the shoulders and chest, the result is only shallow breaths at a cost of considerable effort. Alternatively, the muscular floor to the thoracic cavity can be used. When this large muscle, the diaphragm (which rests above the abdomen) is depressed, large quantities of air enter the lungs. When it is raised, an even pressure can be maintained resulting in a smooth, steady and, when required, sustained supply of air to the voice.

Let us consider how we can develop this diaphragmatic breathing.

The Necessity for Relaxation

How often is a person completely relaxed? Upon reflection the likely answer is that it very seldom happens. If we want to learn how to use the diaphragm for breathing, then we need to know how to relax fully. Lie down on a firm surface and try to relax every muscle in turn. Begin from the feet and, little by little, move toward the head relaxing each group of muscles in turn. Keep the eyes closed and concentrate on the progressive relaxation. This exercise takes several minutes, but if successfully performed it can induce a satisfying sense of physical and mental well-being.

Try to imitate the relaxed breathing of a baby dropping off to sleep. Their method of breathing is typically diaphragmatic, the shoulders are still and the abdomen rises and falls gently. Once we have discovered how to breathe evenly and regularly in this way, we can go on to increase gradually the duration, the capacity and the control of our breathing. The transition from inspiration to expiration is unhurried, and we discover a degree of physical and mental relaxation. In fact, the techniques of yoga exploit this diaphragmatic form of breathing for just this reason.

To test that you are successfully achieving the desired form of breathing, place your hand gently above the abdomen; the slight rise and fall which should be should be discernible as air is first inhaled and then exhaled will confirm that the diaphragm is being used.

Continue the exercise while still keeping the eyes closed, but now begin to allow the breath to make small sounds. This initial sound-making will increase awareness of what actually happens and introduces you to correct sound production. Having mastered diaphragmatic breathing, use it to improve the art of singing. Remember that this technique requires a relaxed posture. If sitting to sing, the legs should not be crossed; when standing, the feet should be set slightly apart so that the body weight is comfortably distributed and the stance is firm. Good voice production always requires proper breath control.

Exercises for Breath Control

- Inhale deeply with the mouth closed, while taking care to keep the shoulders still. Without any strain, hold the breath for a moment and then exhale slowly and, at the same time, sing the syllable "ma" on a note that is comfortable within the range.

- Repeat the exercise with the hand on the abdomen to confirm that the breathing is correct, but this time think carefully about the sound to be made—the pitch, the intensity, the color etc.—before singing it. In other words, let the sound happen first in the imagination and only then in reality in the throat and the mouth.

- Continue by inhaling, holding the breath briefly and then singing but, with each repetition, extend the period the chosen note is sustained.

- Develop the exercise by repeating the above, but choose a note a little higher than the original.

- After a little practice on the higher note repeat the procedure on a lower note.

Vary the exercises by changing the vowel sound using instead syllables like "may," "me," "moo," "mo."

Never strain or overwork the voice. Better to work comfortably and always in a relaxed manner for a few minutes everyday than to struggle for half a day and be unable to sing for a week.

How to Place the Voice

Once you have begun developing the art of breathing correctly (and all singing depends on this), the next step is to discover the right way of placing the voice. This means discovering how the vocal apparatus produces the best sounds. The aim in placing the voice is to develop an awareness of how to adjust the various resonators so as to produce, in a natural way, on all the vowels the ideal tone for each individual voice.

Let us start with the vowel sounds. First, place the fingers lightly on the cheeks and the throat, and then sing through the main vowel sounds - u, o, a, i, e. (note that this is not the alphabetical order). Sound the U as in "blue," the O as in "so," the A as in "baa," the I as in "tribe," and the E as in "be." Doing this brings about an awareness that each sound requires different positionings of the jaw, the tongue, and the lips. It also produces a sensation that the placing of these sounds, uttered in this sequence, moves from the back of the mouth to the front.

Spoken English, of course, does not confine itself to just the five sounds given above but employs long and short versions of each vowel as well as a whole range of intermediate sounds. In addition, there are the diphthongs with their own subtle variations.

Next sing the same vowel sounds, but this time preface them with a sustained "m" sound, i.e., "moo," "mow," "ma," "my" and "me." Before moving from the humming sound onto the vowel, gently place the fingers on the area around the base of the nose and the upper lip; you should experience a slight vibration, even a tickling sensation. Feeling this vibration confirms that the sound is well placed. An extension of this exercise is to substitute an "n" for the initial "m" and sustaining it for a moment before moving to the chosen vowel.

Having learned how to position the voice, our intention should be to maintain this forward placing by constant awareness and regular practice.

Some Exercises for the Vowels

Although, as noted earlier, we actually use far more than the five vowel sounds identified above, for the purpose of exercise we may concentrate on these basic sounds.

- Sing through the vowels in order, on the same note and without pausing to take a breath during the exercise.
- Repeat but sing the vowels in the reverse order. (Notice how the shape of the face changes with each vowel. Take care always to remain relaxed—tension will destroy the tone.)
- Having begun on a note that is easiest to sing in a relaxed manner, gradually extend the range, up and down, while maintaining the same degree of relaxation.
- Identify the vowel sound with which the most pleasing tone is associated,and endeavor to extend this timbre or quality to the other vowel sounds.
- As the control of the diaphragmatic breathing increases, begin to extend the time given to each vowel.

Some Exercises for the Consonants

Whereas "m" and "n" do have vocal sound and can be used to bring the voice forward, the other consonants have no such sound and cannot be sung. They are made audible before the vowel sound is given voice or, when they occur in the middle of a word, they must interrupt with their independent sounds. When they occur at the end of a word, they can only be sounded when the voice has ceased. They need, however, to be clear, crisp, and audible.

By exercising on the various consonants, try to become aware of their individual qualities and their differing demands upon lips, teeth, and tongue.

- Sing through the vowels in turn, placing before each of them a chosen consonant.
- Repeat using a different consonant. It is helpful to use first an explosive sound like b, d, or f etc. and then its softer, corresponding sound p, t, or v.
- In a similar manner, sing the vowels, with or without an initial consonant but placing a consonant at the end.

- Vary the exercise by changing the final consonant while retaining the same vowel, e.g., God, got, gone; Lord, laws, lore; fear, feed, feet, etc.

- Sing, on a monotone, any well-known, alliterative sentences like "Lucy Locket lost her pocket" or "Bob Becket"s baby bounces and bawls." Make up your own, but remember that their purpose is to develop fluency and clarity.

Always pay particular attention to the final consonant. Do not sing it until the note on which the vowel is being sung has received its due measure, but do not neglect it.

As with the suggestions for improving breathing, take care not to tire the voice. Do not attempt all the exercises at once but concentrate on one particular aspect of voice production at a time. Develop the various skills systematically.

Refining the Voice

Remember that the whole person is involved in the act of singing; the heart, the mind, and the body must all be engaged. Although great energy is called for, every care must be taken to avoid straining or forcing the voice. Be comfortable.

What follows are some ways in which the quality of singing can be improved.

- **Preparation**. Inhale before, not at the start of the phrase of music.

- **Intonation**. To ensure a true intonation it is useful to think of the required sound and to place it physically before uttering it. To monitor your intonation, try recording it,and then listen carefully to the playback,or ask a patient friend to listen and comment.

- **Attention to breathing**. Take care to sing in phrases, breathing, as far as possible, at the natural points of punctuation in the text. In the same way that we breathe during speech, take up only sufficient air for the required purpose. Too great an intake creates the problem of getting rid of the excess just when further breath needs to be taken.

- **Quality or timbre of the voice**. Regularly use the brief exercises given above for the placing of the voice. Take care not to develop too nasal a sound, while still making sure that a forward tone is used. To check that this is not happening, sing a warm vowel, like "aah" and sustain it while opening and closing the nostrils—any change in timbre indicates that the tone is too nasal in quality. Further exercises for breathing and placing should correct the fault.

- **Falsetto singing**. Some people can extend the upper range of their voices by employing a technique that uses the resonance cavities of the head to raise the pitch at which they naturally sing. As the name implies, this is a "false" voice, and it should be used only if fully controlled.

All the suggestions offered here focus on the individual voice but, it should be noted, much of what has been said can be applied briefly and with tact to improving the performance of a choir. Only one or two of the exercises should be used, and then for only two or three minutes. Choose a particular vocal aspect of the choir's work that may need some attention and, under the guise of a quick "warm-up" prior to the rehearsal proper, apply the appropriate remedy.

Classification of Voices

In order to organize the groupings within the choir correctly, we need to understand the ways in which voices are classified. To do this we need to be aware that two elements have to be considered; the first is the pitch and range at which the voice can be comfortably used; the second is the general timbre of the voice. As to this last point it must be understood that although two voices may sing notes at similar pitch, the quality of the notes will be different if they are in the middle range or at the limits of the voice.

The differences in the size of the resonators and the length of the vocal cords are responsible for differences in the compass of the voices, as between children and adults and between men and women. Children's and women's voices are higher and generally clearer than men's voices.

Sometimes a voice cannot easily be classified; the reason may be a limited range; in such a case further training will be necessary to extend the range without straining the voice. On the other hand, the singer may be placing the voice incorrectly; in this case careful diagnosis and remedial work will be required.

Patience, persistence, and practice must be the guiding rules. Improvements can only be made slowly, but they are always possible.